FID[

QUAE[

INTELLECTUM

Medieval philosophy from Augustine to Ockham

edited by S.J. Tester

Published by

BRISTOL CLASSICAL PRESS (U.K.)

and

BOLCHAZY-CARDUCCI PUBLISHERS
(U.S.A.)

RUMRLT 4

This is the fourth title in the
Reading University Medieval and
Renaissance Latin Texts Series.
It was prepared for publication by
Keith Bate, General Editor of the
series, after the death of Jim Tester.

Printed in Great Britain by:
Antony Rowe Ltd., Chippenham

First published 1989

U.K.

Bristol Classical Press
226 North Street
Bedminster
Bristol BS3 1JD

ISBN 1-85399-043-4

U.S.A.

Bolchazy-Carducci Publishers
1000 Brown Street, Unit 101
Wauconda
IL 60084

ISBN 0-86516-221-2

CONTENTS

This book, on a subject very close to Jim Tester's heart, was completed just before his death. He worked with great fortitude to complete it during his final debilitating illness. I am proud that Bristol Classical Press is able to publish it as a tribute to the memory of a humane teacher and much loved colleague.

John H. Betts
General Editor
Bristol Classical Press

PREFACE

When in the fifth century the Roman administration disappeared from Western Europe and North Africa, the Roman schools also mostly disappeared, at least outside Italy. In the barbarian kingdoms which succeeded the Empire the Church, with many of its bishops drawn from the old administrative classes, was one of the most important agents in providing that continuity between the ancient world and the medieval which is in many ways more important than the break. Christians had from the beginning adopted and adapted the languages of the Empire, Greek and Latin, for their own purposes and in the West produced what is properly known as Christian Latin. This was the language of all the writers represented in this book; but most of these extracts involve us in only one part of Christian Latin, the language of philosophy. There were three stages in the making of philosophical Latin. The first was in the period of Lucretius and Cicero. In passing on Greek philosophy to their Roman contemporaries they had to make a new language, adapting Latin meanings and transliterating or translating Greek terms, to say what they needed to say. The second stage was in the time from the middle of the fourth century to the early sixth. The most important author was Boethius, who continued the process of the conscious creation of the philosophical vocabulary in his translations, commentaries and original works on the liberal arts. The third period, and the most productive of new words, was the twelfth and thirteenth centuries, when all the wealth of Aristotle and the Arabs had to be put into Latin. Until there is published a sound dictionary of philosophical Latin or medieval Latin generally, one can only guess at the age and provenance of 'new' words. In the notes to these extracts words are not remarked on if they occur in Lewis and Short's *Latin Dictionary* with the meanings they have in our authors. Comment is made if there is a significant change or extension of meaning.

So far as syntax is concerned, only the first, or first few, occurrences of any late or medieval construction are commented upon. Two examples are the expression of reported speech by the use of *quod* or *quia* with a finite verb, and the confusion of the verbals in *-ndum* with the consequent almost total disappearance of the Classical rules. The 'quality' of the Latin - meaning the closeness to somewhat notional Classical norms - varies greatly not only from age to age but from author to author in the same period. To none of these writers was Latin a 'cradle-tongue': all learnt their Latin at school. Since they learnt little else, they learnt more Latin than most of us do; and it was the language in which they thought and disputed and taught and worshipped. So they do not always obey the rules of the Latin grammarians - they are pretty wayward, for example, in their use and non-use of the subjunctive - but they do for the most part try to say what they mean, and sometimes they do it clearly and beautifully. When they are obscure, it is often because what they are trying to say is very difficult.

The period covered by this book is the usual one in books on medieval philosophy, from Augustine to Ockham, a thousand years. There are good reasons for this. There is virtually no Christian philosophy before Augustine, and after the mid-fourteenth century theology and Church politics and reform took up the minds of learned men, until the new learning produced a new philosophy in the seventeenth century. Not that there was no continuity: one cannot properly understand Descartes without the Scholastics. But it makes sense to stop with Ockham.

Augustine stands at the beginning in every way. It is almost true to say that there has been no Christian thinker in the West since the fifth century unaffected by him. Certainly no medieval thinker escaped his influence. His works filled shelves in every monastic and cathedral library. As important, he made philosophy respectable for the Christian, since it was but part of that quest for wisdom and understanding incumbent on a rational creature. *Fides Quaerens Intellectum* is a title of Anselm's making, and it encapsulates his Augustinism. The writers in this book are not trying to prove anything to unbelievers - at least not generally or primarily; only to understand what they believe.

After Augustine and Boethius laid the foundations there was a period of such political turmoil that there was little room for reflective thought until the Carolingian revival of learning in the ninth century. But in the interval two events of very great importance occurred. First, the forces of a new, militant faith, Islam, born in Arabia in 622, conquered the Middle East, North Africa, South Italy and Sicily, and much of Spain. Their courts and schools were to play a very important part in that recovery of Greek science and mathematics and of Aristotle which changed the forms and directions of Western European thought in the twelfth and thirteenth centuries. Second, St. Benedict founded his monastery and wrote his *Rule* and the Benedictine Order was born. With Benedict and Gregory the Great we are clearly out of late antiquity and into the Middle Ages.[1] The efforts of Charlemagne and his successors to improve the standard of education - i.e. Latinity - of their clergy, which were not wholly successful, did however encourage the schools to grow in number and size, and in the centuries that followed more stable and economically improved conditions allowed that flowering, still based firmly on the old Roman legacy of late antiquity, known as the Twelfth Century Renaissance, which overlaps that rediscovery of Aristotle already referred to. Abelard was the last of the early medieval thinkers, having available to him no other sources than had been available to his predecessors for seven hundred years. But by the power of his intellect and the originality of his mind he set himself at the beginning of the new thought already moving in the schools. Not only did he have much to do with the creation of the method of disputation and instruction, but he also stood at the head of that tradition of confident questioning, of trust in and reliance on the powers of reasoning, of dialectic, which so horrified Bernard of Clairvaux and which lasted until the early fourteenth century. In addition to this, Abelard was a major cause of that great gathering of students in Paris which became the first true university in Europe. From the beginning of the twelfth century western philosophy was developed in the schools of Paris, Oxford and others by the schoolmen; and because it was all in the same Catholic Christian tradition, in the same Latin language, and in the same forms, and because masters and students could and did move from school to school, it had a unity despite its inner diversity which makes it reasonable to call it Scholasticism.

The intention of this book is to represent some of the most important contributors to the development of medieval Christian philosophy, to give the reader some taste of the language they used, and to introduce some of the points at which Christian belief touched most evidently on philosophical thinking, where faith most sought - and seeks - understanding.

1 For an interesting indication how conscious the transition was in some men's minds, see S. Morrison, *Politics and Script,* Oxford 1972, esp.ch.3.

BIBLIOGRAPHY

A.H. Armstrong and R.A. Markus, *Christian Faith and Greek Philosophy*, London 1960.

G. Leff, *Medieval Thought from Saint Augustine to Ockham*, Harmondsworth 1958.

D. Knowles, *The Evolution of Medieval Thought*, London 1962.

F.C. Copleston, *A History of Medieval Philosophy*, London 1972. (The best book to begin with.)

F.C. Copleston, *A History of Philosophy; Vol 2 Augustine to Scotus* (1950); *Vol 3 Ockham to Suarez* (1953).

[Cf. also N. Kretzmann, A. Kenny, J. Pinborg, *The Cambridge History of Later Medieval Philosophy*, Cambridge 1982]

1. SAINT AUGUSTINE

St. Augustine was a North African from Tagaste, near Madaura, the native town of Apuleius, where he was educated before going on to the 'university' of Carthage, first as a student and then as a teacher of rhetoric. He died at the age of 76 in 430, while Genseric and his Vandals besieged his episcopal city of Hippo Regius, where he had been bishop for 35 years. During those years, despite the heavy labours of office, he poured out a constant stream of writings - controversial works against various heresies and against the Manichees (to which sect he had himself belonged before his conversion in 387 in Milan, where he was Rhetor and St. Ambrose was bishop); a great number of letters and sermons and commentaries on the Scriptures; works on the sacraments and aspects of belief, and the great work *On the Trinity;* and the two books by which he is most widely known, the *Confessions* and *The City of God.*

Few writers outside Scripture have had so much influence on the thought of succeeding ages in the West as had St. Augustine, and it is fair to say that no one who has not read those last two works, or at least the *Confessions,* will achieve a real understanding of the 'medieval mind'. For medieval thought even in the heyday of Aristotelianism was always strongly coloured by its Augustinian heritage. Philosophically that heritage was broadly Platonic or rather Neoplatonist. St. Augustine came to his Christian belief via Neo-platonism, and the system of Plotinus influenced his own doctrines. One of the two major effects of his work on later thought was due to this philosophical bias: he gave to later ages a specifically Platonic approach which was not broken down (or at least weakened) until after the great arguments of the thirteenth century. The other, and perhaps greater effect of his thought, was due to his own conception of philosophy, of the intellectual aspect of his religion; which was itself due to his own experience. For Augustine, in an historical as well as in a theoretical sense, faith preceded understanding. From this cardinal fact of his experience, described fully in his *Confessions,* is derived the character of his thought. Faith is a gift of God; that gift once received, the mind can try, aided by the light of reason, which is the light of Christ the Teacher, to understand the content of faith. Not only can it try, but it must try, since we are bound as rational creatures to seek to understand what we believe; blind faith is not enough.

But as God is the giver of faith so he is the ground of our understanding. From whatever point the mind starts in its search for understanding, the end and beginning are always in God. Which is why there can be no setting-out as a system of Augustine's philosophy. God is Alpha and Omega, the beginning and the end, and the system is a circle, with God as circumference and centre. So it seems that Augustinism is founded on a *petitio principii:* first you must believe that which later, only because you believe you are aided by grace, you must try to understand and can understand: 'for understanding is the reward of faith; do not seek, then, to understand in order that you may believe, but believe, that you may reach understanding'. You do not prove, but understand, what you believe. You do not believe in God in order to prove that he exists; you may show that the belief in God's existence is a rational belief, but that is different. You believe in God in order that, so far as is possible for a human mind, you may understand God and his works, you may construct a theology and a philosophy. Only these two are not separate for Augustine, nor is either separated from living. Faith is active, faith is a way of living, a way of understanding; and understanding, knowledge of God's truth, in turn is a way of living, a way of believing. St. Augustine heard Christ say 'I am the way, and the truth and the life', and for him all these were truly one, and were God.

This is Augustine's legacy, of faith as the ground and the goal of understanding. Later ages might rationalize the relations between faith and reason, and divide theology from philosophy, but they were the Ages of Faith, and the makers of those distinctions had not known the turning from pagan night to the light of Christ that made Augustine one of the great saints. He took philosophy to be literally 'the love of wisdom'; and Wisdom is Christ; so philosophy and theology are one pursuit, and one of the marks of the Augustinian tradition is the inability, the refusal, to separate the two. Behind all the philosophy of the Middle Ages sound the words of Augustine: *crede ut intellegas.* Always it is faith first, and then it is faith which seeks understanding.

Another keynote of Augustinism might be called its 'existentialist' basis. His thought is derived directly from his own inner experience; which is why the reading of the *Confessions* is essential for the student of that thought. Always Augustine looked within for truth. His book *On the Trinity* is, like the *Confessions*, full of deep psychological insights. And in both he worries over the problem of time, of the transitory nature of our experience, and the eternal wholeness of God. Almost every book written since on 'the problem of time' quotes the lines from the *Confessions:* 'What, then, is time? So long as no one asks me I know; but if I try to explain to someone who does ask me, I don't know'. Book XI of the *Confessions* is one of the earliest and most important discussions of the problem. And there is, as will be seen, a direct and close link between Augustine's arguments and the Boethian definition of eternity in the second extract of his.

BIBLIOGRAPHY

The best life and introduction in English is Peter Brown's *Augustine of Hippo*, London 1967, which has a splendid bibliography; but the older biography, Gustave Bardy's *Saint Augustin*, 6th ed., Paris 1946, is somehow closer to its subject. *A Monument to St. Augustine*, London 1930, is an interesting collection of essays in commemoration of his fifteenth centenary. Etienne Gilson's *Introduction à l'étude de Saint Augustin*, 3rd ed., Paris 1949, is interesting, but the best single work on Augustine is still Eugène Portalié's old article in the *Dictionnaire de Théologie Catholique*, now translated and published as *A Guide to the Thought of St. Augustine*, 1960.

1. St Augustine: Faith and Reason
In Joannis Evangelium Tract.XXIX,6. ed. R. Willems,
Corpus Christianorum, Series Latina XXXVI, 1954

Si intelleximus, Deo gratias! si quid autem parum
intellexit, fecit homo quo usque potuit, cetera videat
3   unde speret. Forinsecus ut operarii possumus plantare
et rigare, sed Dei est incrementum dare (1 Cor.3,6).
Mea, inquit, *doctrina non est mea, sed eius qui misit*
6   *me.* Audiat consilium, qui dicit: 'Nondum intellexi'.
Magna quippe res et profunda cum fuisset dicta, vidit
utique ipse Dominus Christus hoc tam profundum
9   non omnes intellecturos, et in consequenti dedit
consilium. Intellegere vis? crede; Deus enim per
Prophetam dixit:*nisi credideritis, non intellegetis* (Isai.
12   7,9 sec.LXX). Ad hoc pertinet quod etiam hic Dominus secutus adiunxit: *si quis voluerit voluntatem eius*
facere, cognoscet de doctrina, utrum ex Deo sit an ego
15   *a meipso loquar.* Quid est hoc *si quis voluerit volunt-*
atem eius facere? Sed ego dixeram: si quis crediderit;
et hoc consilium dederam: si non intellexisti, inquam,
18   crede. Intellectus enim merces est fidei. Ergo noli
quaerere intellegere ut credas, sed crede ut intellegas;
quoniam *nisi credideritis, non intellegetis.* Cum ergo
21   ad possibilitatem intellegendi consilium dederim
obedientiam credendi, et dixerim Dominum Iesum
Christum hoc ipsum adiunxisse in consequenti
24   sententia, invenimus eum dixisse *si quis voluerit*
voluntatem eius facere, cognoscet de doctrina. Quid
est, *cognoscet?* hoc est, intelleget. Quod est autem, *si*
27   *quis voluerit voluntatem eius facere,* hoc est credere.
Sed quia *cognoscet,* hoc est intelleget, omnes intellegunt; quia vero quod ait, *si quis voluerit voluntatem*
30   *eius facere,* hoc pertinet ad credere, ut diligentius
intellegatur, opus est nobis ipso Domino nostro expo-
sitore, ut indicet nobis utrum revera ad credere per-
33   tineat facere voluntatem Patris eius. Quis nesciat hoc
esse facere voluntatem Dei, operari opus eius, id est,
quod illi placet? Ipse autem Dominus aperte alio loco
36   dicit: *hoc est opus Dei ,ut credatis in eum quem ille*

misit (Ioann.6,29). *Ut credatis in eum,* non ut credatis
ei; sed si creditis in eum, creditis ei; non autem con-
39   tinuo qui credit ei, credit in eum. Nam et daemones
credebant ei, et non credebant in eum. Rursus etiam
de apostolis ipsius possumus dicere, credimus Paulo,
42   sed non credimus in Paulum; credimus Petro, sed
non credimus in Petrum. *Credenti* enim *in eum*
qui iustificat impium, deputatur fides eius ad iustitiam
45   (Rom.4,5). Quid est ergo credere in eum? Credendo
amare, credendo diligere, credendo in eum ire, et eius
membris incorporari. Ipsa est ergo fides quam de
48   nobis exigit Deus: et non invenit quod exigat, nisi
donaverit quod inveniat.Quae fides, nisi quam defin-
ivit alio loco apostolus plenissime dicens: *Neque*
51   *circumcisio aliquid valet neque praeputium, sed fides*
quae per dilectionem operatur (Gal.5,6)? Non qualis-
cumque fides, sed *fides quae per dilectionem oper-*
54   *atur;* haec in te sit, et intelleges de doctrina.Quid enim
intelleges? Quia *doctrina* ista *non est mea, sed eius qui*
misit me: id est, intelleges, quia Christus Filius Dei,
57   qui est doctrina Patris, non est ex seipso, sed Filius
est Patris.

Notes

1.   **intelleximus:** a pure present perfect: 'have understanding'; cf. *perii* - 'I am undone', and *memini* - 'I
have recollected, I remember'.
si quid: if this reading is correct, and not *si quis* as
the Migne text has it, then *homo* must be taken as the
subject, and the sentence translated:'If a man has
understood anything insufficiently well, but has done
what he can..'. If however *si quis* is read, then *homo*
can be taken, as seems more natural, as stressing the
fact that he is *homo* not *Deus* : 'has done all that a
man can'.

2.   **quo usque:** usually written as one word. Used here
metaphorically, 'as far as', 'as much as'; cf. Boethius
DeTrin.praef.25: *artibus..finibus est constitutus, quo-*
usque potest via rationis accedere, which illustrates

the transition from the classical spatial sense to the metaphorical.

3. **forinsecus:** metaphorical: 'outwardly'. In CL only literally and spatially, meaning 'out of doors'.

5. *mea..doctrina* etc. John 7,16.

7. **fuisset dicta:** the CL past participle and *fui, fueram* makes a true perfect or pluperfect passive: *amatus fui* - 'I have been loved (and am no longer)'; cf. Cic. *De Div.* I,34, 74: *arma quae fixa in parietibus fuerant, ea sunt humi inventa.* In later Latin the distinction between these and the normal perfect and pluperfect passives is obscured, as here, where *fuisset = esset* . This tendency may have been encouraged by the popular substitution of the analytical compound *amatus sum* in which the participle is simply a timeless, passive adjective, and the auxiliary bears all the temporal sense, for the synthetic, simple present passive *amor* .

9. **in consequenti:** sc. *sententia* as in line 24 - 'verse'.

11. **Prophetam:** in the language of the Latin Fathers *propheta* alone is used to refer to an OT author, especially Isaiah; as *Apostolus* tends to mean St. Paul and later in the Middle Ages *Philosophus* means Aristotle and *Commentator* Averroes. The word *propheta* itself is from the Greek *prophetes* 'a fore-teller', first used in Latin by the pagan authors Apuleius and Macrobius.

12. **sec.LXX:** = *secundum Septuaginta* . LXX is the abbreviation used for the Septuagint, a Greek trans-lation of the Hebrew OT said to have been made by 72 (not in fact 70) scholars for Ptolemy Philadelphus (285-246 BC) at Alexandria, but probably made there at various times in the 3rd and 2nd centuries BC. The Vulgate and the Authorized Version have *non perma-nebitis,* 'ye shall not be established'; the Old Latin version which Augustine is using, one of the trans-lations of the Scriptures in use until St. Jerome's Vulgate Latin Bible became standard in the 8th and 9th centuries, follows the Septuagint, which has *sunête.* The confusion arose from similar verbs in

Hebrew, and the Syriac also has 'understand'. In the
form in which we have it in this passage it is a favou-
rite quotation of Augustine's, for obvious reasons.
etiam hic: 'in this very passage', i.e. the passage
from St. John's Gospel on which Augustine is
commenting.

16. **sed ego dixeram:** pluperfect = aorist (simple past),
as frequently in early Latin. 22 examples are quoted
from Plautus in C.E. Bennett's *Syntax of Early
Latin*, a useful work for the better understanding of
the syntax of early medieval Latin. Cf. also Propertius
I,12,11: *non sum ego qui fueram* , where *fueram* =
fui 'was, but am no longer'.

18. **intellectus:** this word has the same set of meanings
as the English word 'understanding': (a) the *act* of
comprehension; e.g. Tac.*Ann*. 6,36: *quis neque boni
intellectus neque mali cura*; a meaning derived from its
meaning of perception by the senses, as in Pliny
N.H. 53,116: *nec est intellectus ullus in odore vel
sapore*, by an extension from sense-perception to
mental apprehension. This meaning passes imper-
ceptibly into (b) the *result* of the act, the knowledge
acquired; e.g. Gai. *Inst.* 3,93: *Latini sermonis
intellectum habere;* (c) the *actor*, the intelligence
which understands, the intellect: e.g. Apul. *Dogm.
Plat.* I,p.7,3: *in errorem intellectum inducere.* It is
used in our passage in the second sense. *Intellectus,
intelligentia* are used synonymously in meanings (a)
and (c) frequently in Augustine; cf. *Enarr. in Ps.* 31,
9:*intellectus vel intelligentia.* For a note on the
meanings of *anima, animus, mens, ratio, intellectus,*
etc. in Augustine see Gilson, p.56, note 1.

21. **possibilitatem intelligendi:** *possibilis* first
occurs in Quintilian, but the abstract noun
possibilitas, formed on the analogy of pairs like
humilis - humilitas , is not found before Arnobius and
Martianus Capella (3rd and 4th c. AD) when it is
naturally used with the genitive of the gerund, like
difficultas etc. in Cicero.

22. **obedientiam credendi:** *obed-* for *oboed-*. The

phrase is in apposition to, and explains, *consilium*. In CL *oboedientia* means 'being obedient', and so 'serving': Cic. *Parad. Stoic.* 5,1,35 has *servitus est oboedientia fracti animi*. Later in the Middle Ages it becomes the duty of a monk, monastic discipline (cf. Du Cange s.v.) and here appears to mean 'discipline' or 'duty' generally.

26. quod est autem: referring to the fact 'he will understand': 'which happens if..'.

28. sed quia..omnes intellegunt: *quod* or *quia* (or less commonly *quoniam*) with the indicative, or sometimes the subjunctive as a sort of survival of the sub-oblique construction of CL, is the commonest medieval form of reported speech. Its origins are a little obscure, but it is not enough simply to put it down to imitation of the Greek *hoti* construction. Other reasons apart, the works in which it most commonly occurs were indeed many of them translations from the Greek and therefore intended for readers who knew none, so that unless the construction made sense in Latin it could hardly have been used so freely. A good example of its use, however, in direct imitation of Greek occurs in Priscian's translation of Hermogenes' *Praeexercitamenta* 3: *simiae convenerunt. consiliabantur de urbe condenda. quarum una in medium veniens contionata est, quia oportet ipsas quoque civitatem habere;* here the present tense, *oportet,* gives away the literalness of the translation. *Quod* is used to introduce object clauses in CL; *praetereo quod eam sibi domum delegit* (Cic. *Cluent.* 66,188) ' I pass over the fact that..'. In Plautus, *quia* is also used in this construction: *istuc acerbumst, quia ero carendumst* (*Mil. Glor.* 1210). Later the use is extended to include the construction after verbs of saying and thinking, but not certainly in literature before Petronius, and it is commoner from the 4th c. onwards. Lactantius first uses *quoniam* in the same way, but it is never as frequent as *quod* or *quia.* The use of this construction in the Latin transations of the NT, where certainly Greek *hoti,* which shares so many meanings with *quod,* had some influence, encouraged its spread in Christian literature. Apart from occasional reminders, no further comment on this construction will appear in these notes.

36. *ut credatis:* a jussive subjunctive; see L.& S., *ut* II C i(a), for examples of the use of *ut* 'in clauses which, if independent, would take the imperative mood, often rendered by the infinitive in English'. *in eum:* in CL *credere* is normally used with the dative. In Seneca (*Ep.* 95,50 and 97,6) and in Pliny (*N.H.* 2,3) is found *credere deos*; in the Vulgate and Old Latin versions of the Scriptures *credere in* with the accusative or ablative. So early Latin Christians had four constructions to hand, and at first no distinction was made between them, any more than was made between the various constructions with the Greek *pisteuein,* 'believe', found in the *Koine,* the common Greek spoken from one end of the Mediterranean to the other, and all used in the NT, some possibly in imitation of Hebrew-Aramaic constructions. In Cyprian (200-258 AD) no distinction was yet made in Latin, but Lactantius (d.325 AD) makes the distinction which is explicit here and elsewhere in Augustine. Examples from Augustine are: *Enarr.in. Ps.* 77,8: *hoc est etiam credere in Deum, quod utique plus est quam credere Deo; Sermo* 144,2,2:*sed multum interest, utrum quisque credat ipsum Christum, et utrum credat in Christum. nam ipsum esse Christum et daemones crediderunt. ille enim credit in Christum, qui et sperat in Christum et diligit Christum. nam si fidem habet sine spe et sine dilectione, Christum esse credit, non in Christum credit. Credere Deum* , in Augustine, then, is to believe that God exists; *credere Deo* is to believe God; *credere in Deum* is to believe in God. For the concomitant love of and movement towards God, cf. Thomas Aquinas, *Comm. in Ep. Rom.* 4,1: *credere in Deum demonstrat ordinem fidei in finem, qui est per caritatem; nam credere in Deum est credendo in Deum ire, quod*

caritas facit. (See *'Credere in Deum* ' by Christine
Mohrmann in *Mélanges Joseph de Ghellinck,*
Gembloux 1951, I,277ff.; reprinted in Christine
Mohrmann, *Etudes sur le Latin des Chrétiens,* I,
Rome 1961, 195-203.)

43. **credenti enim.*fides eius*:** *deputare,* to allot or
destine someone to something:'his faith is set down
to (as) righteousness'. The possessive dative *credenti*
is picked up and the possession repeated in the
genitive *eius.*

45. **credendo:** a use of the ablative of the gerund common in later Latin in which the ablative has only a
weak temporal sense and the gerund is equivalent to a
present participle. Cf. Sallust, *Jug.*103,2: *Bocchus,
seu reputando (= seu reputans) .. seu admonitus* etc.

46. **amare..diligere:** no clear distinction can be made
between these two verbs, or between their Greek
equivalents, *philein* and *agapan,* at least in Christian
writings. *Amare, philein* are words used in all, even
the lower, senses; *diligere, agapan* include the ideas
of respect and reverence, but then so might the other
two in a particular context. That *amare* and *diligere*
were practically synonymous for Augustine is shown
by his discussion of the uses of the two verbs in John
21,15ff. in *Civ. Dei* 14,7.

46. **in eum ire:** referring to the Mystical Body of Christ,
of which we are members; cf. John 17,21; I Cor. 12,
2 and many other places in Paul's letters. Cf. also the
texts quoted in the note to line 36.

47. **de nobis:** for the earlier *a* or *ab* with *exigere,* though
Aulus Gellius already has *exigitur de me* in the 2nd c.
But *de* is in the 4th c. acquiring the more general
sense of 'from' or 'of'.

50. **apostolus:** a borrowing from Greek, 'one who is
sent'; cf. note on *propheta ,* line 11.
dicens: a more or less redundant participle introducing the quotation, possibly taken over from the
Hebrew idiom used by Jerome in his version of the
Bible; but cf. Suet. *De Gramm.* 4: *eosdem litteratores*

*vocitatos Messala Corvinus in quadam epistola
ostendit,'nam esse sibi', dicens,'rem cum..'*. This
present participle became so customary a formula for
introducing direct quotation that it was sometimes
used invariably, as in St. Benedict's *Rule,* Prol.51:
audiamus respondentem..dicens 'Qui ingreditur..' .

51. *praeputium*: in a Biblical context only = uncircum-
cision, not being circumcised.

54. **doctrina:** = *verbum*; the generation of an idea in the
mind is an image of the eternal generation of the Word
of God. The complex of ideas has a long history,
before and after the Incarnation, which is well beyond
the scope of these notes.

2. St Augustine: On Time
Confessions XI, 13-15, §§15-18, ed. P. Knöll, CSEL
XXXIII, 1896

At si cuiusquam volatilis sensus vagatur per ima-
gines retro temporum et te, deum omnipotentem et
3   omnicreantem et omnitenentem, caeli et terrae artificem, ab opere tanto, antequam id faceres, per innumerabilia saecula cessasse miratur, evigilet atque
6   adtendat, quia falsa miratur. Nam unde poterant innumerabilia saecula praeterire, quae ipse non feceras,
cum sis omnium saeculorum auctor et conditor? Aut
9   quae tempora fuissent quae abs te condita non essent?
Aut quomodo praeterirent, si nunquam fuissent? Cum
ergo sis operator omnium temporum, si fuit aliquid
12   tempus, antequam faceres caelum et terram, cur
dicitur quod ab opere cessabas? Idipsum enim tempus
tu feceras, nec praeterire potuerunt tempora, antequam
15   faceres tempora. Si autem ante caelum et terram
nullum erat tempus, cur quaeritur, quid tunc faciebas?
Non enim erat tunc, ubi non erat tempus. Nec tu tem-
18   pore tempora praecedis: alioquin non omnia tempora
praecederes. Sed praecedis omnia praeterita celsitudine semper praesentis aeternitatis et superas omnia
21   futura, quia illa futura sunt, et cum venerint, praeterita
erunt; *tu autem idem ipse es, et anni tui non deficient.*
Anni tui nec eunt nec veniunt: isti autem nostri eunt et
24   veniunt, ut omnes veniant. Anni tui omnes simul
stant, quoniam stant, nec euntes a venientibus exclu-
duntur, quia non transeunt: isti autem nostri omnes
27   erunt, cum omnes non erunt. Anni tui dies unus, et
dies tuus non cotidie, sed hodie, quia hodiernus tuus
non cedit crastino; neque enim succedit hesterno. Hod-
30   iernus tuus aeternitas: ideo coaeternum genuisti, cui
dixisti: *ego hodie genui te.* Omnia tempora tu fecisti et
ante omnia tempora tu es, nec aliquo tempore non erat
33   tempus. Nullo ergo tempore non feceras aliquid, quia
ipsum tempus tu feceras. Et nulla tempora tibi coaeterna sunt, quia tu permanes; at illa si permanerent,
36   non essent tempora. Quid est enim tempus? Quis hoc

facile breviterque explicaverit? Quis hoc ad verbum de
illo proferendum vel cogitatione conprehenderit? Quid
39   autem familiarius et notius in loquendo commemor-
amus quam tempus? Et intelligimus utique, cum id
loquimur, intelligimus etiam, cum alio loquente id
42   audimus. Quid est ergo tempus? Si nemo ex me
quaerat, scio; si quaerenti explicare velim, nescio:
fidenter tamen dico scire me, quod, si nihil praeteriret,
45   non esset praeteritum tempus, et si nihil adveniret,
non esset futurum tempus, et si nihil esset, non esset
praesens tempus. Duo ergo illa tempora, praeteritum
48   et futurum, quomodo sunt, quando et praeteritum iam
non est et futurum nondum est? Praesens autem si
semper esset praesens nec in praeteritum transiret,
51   non iam esset tempus, sed aeternitas. Si ergo praesens, ut tempus sit, ideo fit, quia in praeteritum
transit, quomodo et hoc esse dicimus, cui causa, ut
54   sit, illa est, quia non erit, ut scilicet non vere dicamus
tempus esse, nisi quia tendit non esse. Et tamen dicimus longum tempus et breve tempus neque hoc nisi
57   de praeterito aut futuro dicimus. Praeteritum tempus
longum verbi gratia vocamus ante centum annos,
futurum itidem longum post centum annos, breve
60   autem praeteritum sic, ut puta dicamus ante decem
dies, et breve futurum post decem dies. Sed quo pacto
longum est aut breve, quod non est? Praeteritum enim
63   iam non est et futurum nondum est. Non itaque dicamus 'longum est', sed dicamus de praeterito 'longum
fuit', et de futuro 'longum erit'. Domine meus, lux
66   mea, nonne et hic veritas tua deridebit hominem?
Quod enim longum fuit praeteritum tempus, cum iam
esset praeteritum, longum fuit, an ante, cum adhuc
69   praesens esset? Tunc enim poterat esse longum
quando erat, quod esset longum: praeteritum vero iam
non erat; unde nec longum esse poterat, quod omnino
72   non erat. Non ergo dicamus 'longum fuit praeteritum
tempus'; neque enim inveniemus, quid fuerit longum,
quando ex quo praeteritum est non est, sed dicamus
75   'longum fuit illud praesens tempus', quia cum praesens esset, longum erat. Nondum enim praeterierat, ut

non esset, et ideo erat, quod longum esse posset;
78 postea vero quam praeteriit, simul et longum esse
destitit, quod esse destitit.

Notes

1. **volatilis sensus:** 'butterfly mind'. For *volatilis* in
this sense cf. Seneca *Ep.*12,3: *gloria vanum et volatile
quiddam est, auraque mobilius. Sensus* here = understanding, mind; see L.& S. s.v.II B.
2. **retro:** 'in the past', both adverb and adjective, in a
way: the distinction is not always possible, but then it
is a distinction drawn by grammarians. Cf. Horace *C.*
III,29,46 *quodcumque retro est.*
3. **omnicreantem:** this seems to be an Augustinian
invention but it is a natural enough formation, with
many CL and late parallels.
omnitenentem: Tertullian probably made this word
along with so many that did not long survive their
inventor. It had much the same meaning as the   commoner *omnipotens* which, despite attempts to diffe-
rentiate between the two words, eventually drove
omnitenens out.
artificem: Tertullian and Lactantius both used *artifex*
of the Creator, but cf. also the Stoic use with *natura*
as in Cic. *DND* II, 58.
4. **ab opere tanto..cessasse:** for *cessare ab* cf. Livy
IV, 27, 5: *nec cessatum a levibus proeliis est;* and
elsewhere. The origin of Augustine's phrase is the
Vulgate, Gen.2,3.
antequam id faceres: the imperfect subjunctive is
used because of *cessasse,* which is past; the historic
verb always overrides a primary context.
11. **operator:** notice Augustine ringing the changes on
words for 'maker': *artifex, auctor, conditor, operator,*
while he keeps to the Genesis word *facere* for 'make'.
Creare, creator did not supersede all their rivals until
later. *Operator* = 'maker' is a Christian Latin usage.
13. **idipsum:** note, not 'time itself', but 'that time itself',
i.e. the *aliquod tempus* of the previous line. Hence

pluperfect *feceras*.

17. non enim erat tunc: 'there was no "then"'.

19. celsitudine: apart from two instances from Ammianus, all the examples of this metaphorical use of 'height' in the TLL are from Christian writers. Notice the shift in meaning from *praecedis* in line 18 through *praecedis* line 19 to *superas* line 20; though the two uses of *praecedis* include the ideas both of preceding and of being superior (cf. 'precedence').

22. *tu autem*..: Ps.102,27 AV; 101,28 Vulgate.

26. isti autem nostri omnes erunt: ignored in the notes of Montgomery and Gibb, paraphrased or amended in most translations ('will all be ours' in one, 'will all be thine' in another) or translated literally into nonsense, e.g. 'these of ours will all be when all shall cease to be'. What Augustine says is (23 ff.): 'Your years neither go nor come: but these of ours go and come, so that all may come. All your years stand together, because they do stand; nor are those going pushed out by those coming, because they do not pass; but these of ours will be all (sc.complete) when they shall all be past (i.e. be no longer).' The point is that 'all' our years *means* 'all': there will be an end to them, the Judgement. Our years 'move' so that all may come, and when all have come, and are therefore all past, and therefore in a sense do not exist, then that will be *all*.. The *omnes* in *isti autem nostri omnes erunt* in line 26 must be predicative.

29. hodiernus: usually not without *dies*; but Seneca has *sibi crastinum polliceri* 'to promise oneself tomorrow', and *in crastinum* was as old as Plautus. L.& S. are probably wrong to suggest a neuter noun *crastinum*: it was most likely always *crastinus (dies)*, and *hodiernus, hesternus* were used in the same way.

31. *ego hodie genui te*: Ps.2,7.

32. tu es: cf. John 8,58; and the ref. is to Exodus 3,14.

33. nullo..non feceras: not a double negative, but 'in no time therefore did you not make something, because you made time itself'. The pluperfects are probably aorists: cf. note on Extract 1, line 16.

34. coaeterna: probably Tertullian's creation.

36. quis..explicaverit? quis..conprehenderit?: perfect subjunctives expressing the unreality of the idea: 'Surely there is no one who has..'.

38. vel cogitatione: 'even in thought'.

42. si..quaerat, scio; si..velim, nescio: Kühner says that if the if-clause is concessive or adversative, it has the subjunctive with the indicative in the main clause; he quotes Cic. *De Div.* II,108: *si aliquando oculi peccent, tamen..inest in iis vis videndi.*

55. tendit non esse: 'moves toward not being', and getting close to 'tends not to be'.

60. ut puta: *puta = verbi gratia*, 'for example', and the *ut* governs, presumably, *dicamus*; but perhaps the text should read, with most MSS and editors, *dicimus*, in which case *ut puta* is used as in Seneca and late Latin writers, simply to mean 'e.g.'.

66. hominem: 'man' not 'a man' as in the Loeb version.

70. quando erat, quod esset longum: 'when there was such as might be long', 'when there was something to be long'.

74. quando ex quo: 'since from the time when'.

79. quod esse destitit: a good example of *quod* = 'which' and 'because', showing how it can be used for both.

2. BOETHIUS

Anicius Manlius Severinus Boethius was consul at thirty to the Ostrogothic king of Italy, Theodoric, in 510, and later Magister Officiorum, or Secretary, in which post he was succeeded by Cassiodorus, to whom the Middle Ages owed much as a preserver of antiquity. Boethius had received a full Classical education, including Greek language and philosophy; he was virtually the last Western scholar so educated before the Renaissance. His ideal was Plato's philosopher-statesman, and his own life was exemplary in its probity in the service of a great king. Theodoric had a sincere respect , as had so many of the 'barbarians' who overran the Empire in the 5th and 6th centuries, for the Roman tradition, and despite the fact that , like all the Goths, he was an Arian Christian, he dealt tolerantly with his Catholic Italian subjects, saying, according to Cassiodorus: *religionem imperare non possumus, quia nemo cogitur ut credat invitus* (*Variae*, II,27). At least, he was tolerant until his later years, when the fear of an attempt by Justin I in Constantinople to regain Italy caused him not only to persecute the Catholics but to imprison, torture and execute Boethius in about 524 on charges of conspiracy with the Byzantine Emperor and of magic. This last reminds one of similar charges levelled at Gerbert of Aurillac in the 10th century and Roger Bacon in the 13th: all probably due to the same ignorant incomprehension and fear of great learning, especially of a scientific and mechanical kind.

It was in his last year, in prison, that Boethius wrote the *De Consolatione Philosophiae*, which was not only one of the best-loved books of the Middle Ages but enjoyed great popularity with the Platonic revival of the Renaissance. There are English versions by two English sovereigns, Alfred and Elizabeth I, and by Chaucer. It also should be a 'set book' with Augustine's *Confessions* and Benedict's *Rule* for all students of the Middle Ages. In addition to that work, which is essentially Platonic and purely philosophical, containing little indication of Boethius' Christianity, he wrote four or five theological tracts. On philosophy and theology in Boethius see the note on line 43 of the first extract. He composed a number of textbooks on the subjects of the Quadrivium. This was the 'advanced' part of late Classical and Medieval education, comprising Arithmetic, Geometry, Music and Astronomy. The first, elementary, part, called the Trivium (hence our word 'trivial'), was Grammar, Rhetoric and Dialectic (or Logic). Boethius intended to transmit in Latin to his Greekless contemporaries and successors the works of Plato and Aristotle, so far as he could get hold of them, with commentaries designed to show their fundamental agreement. He succeeded in translating and commenting on no more than the logical works of Aristotle (the *Organon* or 'instrument' of philosophy) and its introduction, the *Isagoge* of Porphyry. Until the middle of the 12th century, when translations of Greek works came from Spain and Sicily, all that the Latin west knew of Plato and Aristotle was a part of the *Timaeus* of Plato, partly in the translation of Cicero and partly in that of Chalcidius, accompanied by a commentary; and some of the *Organon*, for although it seems certain that Boethius translated more of Aristotle's logical works, the *Analytics* and the *Topics* were unknown until the 12th century, when their addition to the others converted the *logica vetus* into the *logica nova*. Apart from the importance of the transmission of Aristotle's logic (including the syllogism, in Boethius' own logical writings), one of Boethius' main contributions to medieval and later philosophy was his creation, following Cicero, of a Latin philosophical vocabulary; as before with Cicero, and later in the 12th and 13th centuries, it was in translating Greek works that the need arose to forge a new vocabulary in Latin.

The Platonic character of the *Consolation* has been remarked on already, and Boethius' answer to the problem of God's fore-knowledge and man's freedom is essentially Platonic. The language of his famous definition of eternity, however, and his application of that idea of eternity to the solution of the problem, are his own. Without going into the difficult question as to how far the ancient philosophers had conceived eternity in this timeless way, it must be said that although Plato and the Neoplatonists were aware of a distinction between eternity and endless duration of time, it was not clearly formulated nor was it closely linked with an idea of God. Augustine carried these philosophical notions further in Book XI of the *Confessions*, as we have seen, and verbal echoes show that Boethius was much influenced by these passages. But here he is clearer and has a purpose, applying these ideas of time and eternity to solve a problem which did not exist for the pagan philosophers. For them there was no question of an omnipotent, omniscient God. The problem is raised by the religious doctrines of the creation and man's freedom. God made the world, and knows the world, and he is omniscient. But he also made man free, 'in his own image'. That we are free is as fundamental a dogma of Christianity as that God is omniscient; but how can we reconcile the two? If I say 'Tomorrow I shall either go to London or not go to London', no man knows which half of the disjunction is going to be true, since the answer depends upon many factors including me. But God must know, otherwise he is guessing in the dark as you or I are; and if God knows that, say, the second half will be true tomorrow, am I still a free agent? Is it not predetermined that I shall not go to London? Boethius' answer, based on the distinctions between providence and fate and between eternity and time, is the standard medieval answer at least until the late 13th century, when some thinkers, of whom the greatest was John Duns Scotus, had doubts about it. The problem will come up again in the last extracts.

It must be kept distinct from two separate though allied problems, one theological and the other philosophical. The first concerns God's predestination, which will occupy us in Extract 6. The second is the logical problem of disjunctive propositions in the future: one half of the disjunction, 'either p or not-p' where p is a future proposition, will be true at some time in the future, and is then in some way necessarily true, so that the future seems to be somehow determined. Neither of these is Boethius' problem. He is concerned with reconciling on a philosophical level two seemingly contradictory dogmas, God's omniscience and man's freedom. His answer, which was also that of Thomas Aquinas, rests on the distinction between time, albeit endless, and eternity, which is proper to God.

BIBLIOGRAPHY

The shortest introduction is the article by L. Minio-Paluello, with full bibliography, in the *Dictionary of Scientific Biography*, vol.II, New York 1970, pp.228-36; but the best is now undoubtedly Henry Chadwick's *Boethius:the Consolations of Music, Logic, Theology and Philosophy*, Oxford 1981. The chapter in E.K. Rand's *Founders of the Middle Ages*, (a splendid book), Harvard 1935, H.R. Patch's *The Tradition of Boethius*, Oxford 1935 and H.M. Barrett's *Boethius*, Cambridge 1940 are all useful.
[cf. also *Boethius:his Life, Thought and Influence*, Oxford 1981, a collection of essays edited by M. Gibson]

1. Boethius: Providence and Fate
De Consolatione Philosophiae IV, prose 6, 7-20, ed. G. Weinberger, CSEL 67, 1934

Tunc velut ab alio orsa principio ita disseruit: Omnium generatio rerum cunctusque mutabilium naturarum
3   progressus et, quicquid alio movetur modo, causas, ordinem, formas ex divinae mentis stabilitate sortitur. Haec in suae simplicitatis arce composita multiplicem
6   rebus gerendis modum statuit. Qui modus cum in ipsa divinae intelligentiae puritate conspicitur, providentia nominatur; cum vero ad ea, quae movet atque
9   disponit, refertur, fatum a veteribus appellatum est. Quae diversa esse facile liquebit, si quis utriusque vim mente conspexerit; nam providentia est ipsa illa divina
12   ratio in summo omnium principe constituta, quae cuncta disponit, fatum vero inhaerens rebus mobilibus dispositio, per quam providentia suis
15   quaeque nectit ordinibus. Providentia namque cuncta pariter quamvis diversa, quamvis infinita complectitur, fatum vero singula digerit in motum
18   locis, formis ac temporibus distributa, ut haec temporalis ordinis explicatio in divinae mentis adunata prospectum providentia sit, eadem vero adunatio
21   digesta atque explicata temporibus fatum vocetur.
    Quae licet diversa sint, alterum tamen pendet ex altero; ordo namque fatalis ex providentiae simplicitate
24   procedit. Sicut enim artifex faciendae rei formam mente praecipiens movet operis effectum et, quod simpliciter praesentarieque prospexerat, per temp-
27   orales ordines ducit, ita deus providentia quidem singulariter stabiliterque facienda disponit, fato vero haec ipsa, quae disposuit, multipliciter ac temporaliter
30   amministrat. Sive igitur famulantibus quibusdam pro- videntiae divinis spiritibus fatum exercetur seu anima seu tota inserviente natura seu caelestibus siderum
33   motibus seu angelica virtute seu daemonum varia sollertia seu aliquibus horum seu omnibus fatalis series texitur, illud certe manifestum est immobilem
36   simplicemque gerendarum formam rerum esse provi-

dentiam, fatum vero eorum, quae divina simplicitas
gerenda disposuit, mobilem nexum atque ordinem
39 temporalem.
   Quo fit, ut omnia, quae fato subsunt, providentiae
quoque subiecta sint, cui ipsum etiam subiacet fatum,
42 quaedam vero, quae sub providentia locata sunt, fati
seriem superent; ea vero sunt, quae primae propinqua
divinitati stabiliter fixa fatalis ordinem mobilitatis
45 excedunt. Nam ut orbium circa eundem cardinem sese
vertentium, qui est intimus, ad simplicitatem medie-
tatis accedit ceterorumque extra locatorum veluti cardo
48 quidam, circa quem versentur, exsistit, extimus vero
maiore ambitu rotatus, quanto a puncti media individuitate discedit, tanto amplioribus spatiis explicatur, si
51 quid vero illi se medio conectat et societ, in simplicitatem cogitur diffundique ac diffluere cessat, simili
ratione, quod longius a prima mente discedit,
54 maioribus fati nexibus implicatur ac tanto aliquid fato
liberum est, quanto illum rerum cardinem vicinius
petit. Quodsi supernae mentis haeserit firmitati, motu
57 carens fati quoque supergreditur necessitatem. Igitur
uti est ad intellectum ratiocinatio, ad id quod est id
quod gignitur, ad aeternitatem tempus, ad punctum
60 medium circulus, ita est fati series mobilis ad providentiae stabilem simplicitatem. Ea series caelum ac
sidera movet, elementa in se invicem temperat et
63 alterna commutatione transformat; eadem nascentia
occidentiaque omnia per similes fetuum seminumque
renovat progressus. Haec actus etiam fortunasque
66 hominum indissolubili causarum conexione constrin-
git, quae cum ab immobilis providentiae proficiscatur
exordiis, ipsas quoque immutabiles esse necesse est.
69 Ita enim res optime reguntur, si manens in divina
mente simplicitas indeclinabilem causarum ordinem
promat, hic vero ordo res mutabiles et alioquin temere
72 fluituras propria incommutabilitate coherceat.

Notes

1. **Tunc velut..:** the subject is the lady Philosophia.
3. **movetur:** the so-called passive (actually middle and intransitive) *moveri* is used for the Greek *kineisthai*, to mean 'change' in the most general sense (movement is change of position in space). Aristotle's 'unmoved mover' is an 'unchanged changer'. The English words 'move' and 'change' both have the same capacity as *kinein* and *movere* to be used transitively, in the active and the passive, and intransitively
- in Greek and Latin in the middle voice.
10. **Quae diversa:** i.e. *providentia* and *fatum*.
   utriusque vim: 'the nature of each'; *vis* almost becomes 'nature' in Cicero, especially in the expression *vis et natura*, and by the time of Quintilian the two are synonymous. See L.& S. s.v.II B.
14. **mobilibus:** 'changeable'.
   suis: since it is *suis quaeque..ordinibus, suis* refers to 'all things' not to *providentia*, 'all things, each in its own ordering'.
19. **adunata:** 'made one': largely a Christian writers' word, only found elsewhere in legal writers.
26. **praesentarie:** *praesentarius* is one of the fair number of words which occur in Plautus and early Latin, and then seem not to be used for centuries until found again in later writers - in this case in Aulus Gellius. Were they then 'archaisms', deliberate revivals of old words, or were they popular words that were dropped from literature as 'vulgar' in the Classical period? The adverb *praesentarie* seems to be first used here: 'in the present moment', or possibly 'instantaneously'.
27. **ducit:** 'produces'. The word possibly developed this sense from a military use such as *ducere vallum, ducere fossam*; see L.& S. s.v.I B 6.
28. **singulariter:** as the context shows, not 'one by one' but 'in one act', or 'simply', 'singly'.
   stabiliter: 'in an unchanging way' as opposed to *mobiliter*. The two adverbs correspond to *simpliciter praesentarieque*.

29. temporaliter: literally 'temporally', 'in a temporal way'; not, as it seems in Tertullian, 'temporarily'. Augustine has it in our sense, and opposes it to *aeternaliter, De Trin.*14,1,3.

30. Sive igitur: Boethius' Neoplatonist sources would have suggested the intermediaries, and contemporary Stoicism, Neopythagoreanism, astrology and so on provided other 'explanations' of fate's workings.

33. angelica virtute seu daemonum: 'whether by angelic power or the shifting cunning of demons': *angelus* and *daemon* are both Greek words taken straight into Latin from Scripture. *Daemon*, a good or evil spirit, was already in use in pagan writers, particularly astrologers, where it was the name for one of the 'mundane houses'; *angelus* was purely a Biblical word.

43. primae..divinitati: it was phrases like this, and passages like this extract, with all its pagan philosophical references, which persuaded scholars that Boethius was a pagan himself, until the discovery of a fragment of Cassiodorus proved that he wrote the *Theological Tractates* (See H. Usener, *Anecdoton Holderi*, Leipzig 1877). That he was believed to be a pagan enabled Gibbon to regard him in a friendly light; that he was in fact a Christian forced Christians to explain the 'paganism' of the *Consolation* . The answer to this problem is probably not the 'simple' one proposed by Stewart and Rand in the preface to the Loeb edition: 'In the *Consolation* he is writing philosophy; in the *Tractates* he is writing theology.' That is anachronistic. No distinction was yet made between theology and philosophy except that the latter was pagan, and so was rejected totally by many Christian writers. The distinction was not between theology and philosophy as such, but between Christianity and paganism. And even that was blurred. None of us keeps his 'religious' and other beliefs in separate 'boxes': everything we believe affects everything else. In the 5th and 6th c. (and *a fortiori* , perhaps, in the 4th c.) paganism and Christianity as ideas coexisted in the minds, though probably not as practices in the lives, of many Christians. Boethius' mind was not merely stocked with, but formed by the ancient philosophers. This work is the consolation offered to him in prison by the lady Philosophy, who had been his companion for many years. Modern distinctions are not necessarily applicable. Boethius was a Christian and a philosopher, as many today are Christians and Marxists. And when all is said, Books IV and V of the *Consolation* are Christian enough in argument and tone for anyone not predisposed to regard their author as pagan.

45. ut orbium: the *ut* , 'just as', is picked up by *simili ratione* in line 52.

sese vertentium: the reflexive form does the job of a middle participle, intransitive, whereas Boethius then goes on to use *versentur* . For a middle present participle cf. Virgil *Aen.* 10,362 *rotantia.* The sentence would be better punctuated for English readers at least without the commas on either side of *qui est intimus*: 'for as spheres..the innermost one approaches..'.

49. individuitate: 'indivisibility' (points have position but no magnitude). The word is probably Tertullian's. *Media* is best translated with *puncti*, as a sort of transferred epithet.

62. elementa..temperat: the elements are the four, namely earth, air, fire and water, the proportions of which in anything make its constitution. They were themselves sometimes thought of as mixtures of four fundamental qualities, hot, cold, wet and dry, and therefore could be transformed one into another by rearrangement of the qualities. All this, and the association with the movement of the stars, lies behind alchemy, of course. For a fascinating account of many of the ramifications of this see *Saturn and Melancholy* by R. Klibansky, E. Panofsky and F. Saxl, London 1964.

63. eadem: nominative, sc.*series*. So, too, *haec*, line 65.

67. **immobilis..immutabiles:** clearly synonymous here, meaning 'unchangeable'.
72. **incommutabilitate:** an Augustinian word.
 coherceat: the 'h' merely represents the glottal stop, as frequently between vowels; CL usually reads *coercere* etc.

2. Boethius: Eternity
De Consolatione Philosophiae, V, prose 6, 1-17

Quoniam igitur, uti paulo ante monstratum est,
omne, quod scitur, non ex sua, sed ex comprehen-
3   dentium natura cognoscitur, intueamur nunc, quantum
fas est, quis sit divinae substantiae status, ut quaenam
etiam scientia eius sit, possimus agnoscere. Deum
6   igitur aeternum esse cunctorum ratione degentium
commune iudicium est. Quid sit igitur aeternitas,
consideremus; haec enim nobis naturam pariter
9   divinam scientiamque patefacit. Aeternitas igitur est
interminabilis vitae tota simul et perfecta possessio,
quod ex collatione temporalium clarius liquet. Nam
12   quicquid vivit in tempore, id praesens a praeteritis in
futura procedit, nihilque est in tempore constitutum,
quod totum vitae suae spatium pariter possit amplecti,
15   sed crastinum quidem nondum apprehendit, hester-
num vero iam perdidit; in hodierna quoque vita non
amplius vivitis quam in illo mobili transitorioque
18   momento. Quod igitur temporis patitur condicionem,
licet illud, sicuti de mundo censuit Aristoteles, nec
coeperit umquam esse nec desinat vitaque eius cum
21   temporis infinitate tendatur, nondum tamen tale est, ut
aeternum esse iure credatur. Non enim totum simul
infinitae licet vitae spatium comprehendit atque com-
24   plectitur, sed futura nondum, transacta iam non habet.
Quod igitur interminabilis vitae plenitudinem totam
pariter comprehendit ac possidet, cui neque futuri
27   quicquam absit nec praeteriti fluxerit, id aeternum esse
iure perhibetur idque necesse est et sui compos
praesens sibi semper assistere et infinitatem mobilis
30   temporis habere praesentem.
      Unde non recte quidam, qui, cum audiunt visum
Platoni mundum hunc nec habuisse initium temporis
33   nec habiturum esse defectum, hoc modo conditori
conditum mundum fieri coaeternum putant. Aliud est
enim per interminabilem duci vitam, quod mundo
36   Plato tribuit, aliud interminabilis vitae totam pariter
complexum esse praesentiam, quod divinae mentis

proprium esse manifestum est. Neque deus conditis
39 rebus antiquior videri debet temporis quantitate sed
simplicis potius proprietate naturae. Hunc enim vitae
immobilis praesentarium statum infinitus ille tempo-
42 ralium rerum motus imitatur, cumque eum effingere
atque aequare non possit, ex immobilitate deficit in
motum, ex simplicitate praesentiae decrescit in
45 infinitam futuri ac praeteriti quantitatem et, cum
totam pariter vitae suae plenitudinem nequeat
possidere, hoc ipso, quod aliquo modo numquam
48 esse desinit, illud, quod implere atque exprimere non
potest, aliquatenus videtur aemulari alligans se ad
qualemcumque praesentiam huius exigui volucrisque
51 momenti, quae, quoniam manentis illius praesentiae
quandam gestat imaginem, quibuscumque contigerit,
id praestat, ut esse videantur. Quoniam vero manere
54 non potuit, infinitum temporis iter arripuit eoque
modo factum est, ut continuaret eundo vitam, cuius
plenitudinem complecti non valuit permanendo. Itaque
57 si digna rebus nomina velimus imponere, Platonem
sequentes deum quidem aeternum, mundum vero
dicamus esse perpetuum.
60 Quoniam igitur omne iudicium secundum sui
naturam, quae sibi subiecta sunt, comprehendit, est
autem deo semper aeternus ac praesentarius status,
63 scientia quoque eius omnem temporis supergressa
motionem in suae manet simplicitate praesentiae
infinitaque praeteriti ac futuri spatia complectens
66 omnia, quasi iam gerantur, in sua simplici cognitione
considerat. Itaque si praevidentiam pensare velis,
qua cuncta dinoscit, non esse praescientiam quasi
69 futuri, sed scientiam numquam deficientis instantiae
rectius aestimabis. Unde non praevidentia, sed
providentia potius dicitur, quod porro a rebus infimis
72 constituta quasi ab excelso rerum cacumine cuncta
prospiciat.

Notes

1. **paulo ante:** cf. V, prose 4: *omne enim quod cognoscitur non secundum sui vim sed secundum cognoscentium potius comprehenditur facultatem* . Boethius then gives as an example the apprehension of roundness by sight - *eminus manens totum simul iactis radiis intuetur* - and by touch - *cohaerens orbi atque coniunctus circa ipsum motus ambitum rotunditatem partibus comprehendit.* The kind of knowledge depends partly on the instrument of knowing.

2. **ex sua:** for the use of *ex* ='according to', cf. *ex sententia, ex ingenio*, etc., and see L.& S. s.v.III H.

4. **substantiae:** the words *essentia, substantia, subsistentia*, as translations of the Greek terms *ousia , hypostasis*, are found in Seneca, Tacitus, Quintilian and other authors of the Silver Age, without any clear distinctions in their meanings. When these terms became important in theological discussions on the Trinity in the 4th to 6th centuries, Greek usage favoured a definition of one *ousia* and three *hypostaseis*, but Latin usage remained confused, worse confounded by the introduction of the word *persona* (translating the Greek *prosopon*) so that Trinitarian definitions could read *una essentia, tres substantiae (mia ousia, treis hypostaseis)*, or *una substantia, tres personae (mia ousia, treis prosopa*, but using the other Latin word for *ousia). That substantia = ousia* was shown by the use of *consubstantialis* for the Greek *homoousios*; but *hypostasis* literally translated in its parts into Latin yields *substantia. Subsistentia* and *essentia* both meant *ousia* also, but both could mean 'existence'. The confusion is well illustrated in Augustine, *De Trin.* 5,8; *plerique nostri qui haec Graeco tractant eloquio dicere consuerunt mia ousia, treis hypostaseis, quod est unam essentiam, tres substantias;* 7,4; *sic enim dicunt illi (sc. Graeci) tres substantias, unam essentiam, quemadmodum nos dicimus tres personas, unam essentiam vel substantiam.* And six centuries later in St. Anselm, *Ep*.4,104:

Graeci quidem nomen substantiae, Latini vero nomen
personae; sed ut omnino quod nos ibi intelligimus
per personam, hoc ipsi et non aliud intelligant per
substantiam. Sicut ergo nos dicimus in Deo unam
substantiam esse tres personas, ita illi dicunt unam
personam esse tres substantias, nihil a nobis diverse
intelligentes aut credentes. For a full discussion of the
history of these words see J. de Ghellinck in the
Bulletin du Cange, XVI, 1941, 77ff.
status: from meaning 'state', 'condition', this word
approximates in meaning to *natura* in CL: cf. Lucretius, *De Rer. Nat.* 5, 829; Cic. *Rep.*1, 28, 44; Quint.
3,6 etc. It also has the meaning 'existence' in Cic.
Cael. 29,70; *Sull.* 26, 63; and in Tert. *De Anima* 4.

6. **degentium:** originally always with an accusative -
diem, aetatem, tempus etc. - *degere* is used absolutely, meaning 'to live', in Tacitus, Pliny, Seneca
and later writers.

8. **haec:** presumably referring vaguely to the nature of
aeternitas , the *quid sit*.

9. **Aeternitas igitur..:** every word of this careful
definition is important. Eternity is the *possessio,* the
having, holding, of *vita,* life - not simply existence or
being, but life; it is the *tota possessio*, the possession
of the whole, not part, of life; *simul,* at one instant,
not spread over a period of time, however short; and
perfecta, not incomplete or shared, but perfect; and
not simply of life, but of *interminabilis vita*, life inca-
pable of having any limits or bounds set to it: 'eternity
is the whole, simultaneous and perfect possession of
boundless life'.

12. **vivit:** 'lives', not simply 'is'; perhaps time is only
real for a living being which moves and changes.

13. **nihilque:** for the more normal CL *nec quicquam*:
'and nothing'.

17. **transitorio:** in CL 'affording a passage', as in
Suetonius, of *domus*. It is first used for 'transitory',
'fleeting', in the 3rd c. and is often so used by Jerome
and Augustine. Cassiodorus uses it so of *vita*.

19. **Aristoteles:** *De Caelo* 283b 26: 'neither did the

whole universe come into being nor can it perish'.

20. vitaque eius: beginning a new clause after *licet* and equivalent to *licetque vita eius*.

23. infinitae licet: *licet* is used adverbially in place of CL *quamquam* only after Seneca.

27. id..idque: both must refer to *quod igitur..possidet, cui..fluxerit:* it must always be with itself in the present, the eternal present of God, and possessing itself, completely conscious of itself as always, eternally, in one present moment, holding the whole of time, past, present, and to come, all present in that eternal instant.

31. quidam: it is impossible to say who these were. They were presumably *Platonici* of some kind. The traditional Platonist view, and certainly that of Proclus, was that the world was *genneton* (begotten, brought into being) not temporally but in that it had a cause outside of itself; and that it was coeternal with its maker, since his activity was eternal. Some however, like Atticus and Plutarch, held that the world had a beginning but should have no end. After *quidam* supply *opinantur* or the like, since *putant* follows *qui*.

visum: sc.*esse*. Cf. Plato *Tim.* 28b 2 ff. 'We must consider concerning the universe whether it has always existed, having no beginning (cause?), or came into being and had a beginning (cause?). It came into being; for it is visible and tangible and is material, and all such things are sensible objects, and sensible objects, comprehended by opinion founded on sensation, are only becoming and were brought into being.' Plato leaves it doubtful whether the world has an end or not (though see note on line 57), but it is clearly not eternal in Boethius' sense.

32. initium temporis: 'a beginning in time': *temporis = temporale*. For the use of the genitive cf. CL *id temporis* 'at this moment of time', *hoc noctis* 'at this time of night'. *Tum temporis* is used to mean *eo tempore* in the 2nd c. by Justinus; and cf. *ubi gentium, quoquo gentium*, both from Plautus, and *quoquo* *terrarum*   from Terence, for similar locatival uses of the genitive.

33. **conditori:** though often used for 'Creator', as *condere* for 'to create', perhaps because of pagan Stoic associations such as Seneca's *mundi conditor*, it lost out to *creator, creari.*

47. **hoc ipso, quod:** 'by this very fact, that..', where *quod* introduces an object clause explaining the antecedent demonstrative; a CL construction from which developed its use to introduce object clauses in general.

48. **illud:** a sense-construction (it should grammatically refer to *hunc..statum* in line 40), where it means 'that', i.e. all that has been said of eternity.
    implere atque exprimere: for this use of *implere* = 'to fulfil the office of' or 'to achieve', cf. *implere censorem* in Velleius Paterculus 2,95, and its common use with *officium* in later Latin; cf. also Benedict's *Rule* 2: *(Abbas debet) nomen maioris factis implere.*

52. **quibuscumque:** taken both with *contigerit* and *praestat.* For *contingere* with the dative cf. Caesar *Bell. Gall. I*, 38,5: *ita ut radices montis ex utraque parte ripae fluminis contingant.*

57. **Platonem sequentes:** *Timaeus* 37D ff. The 'pattern' (*paradeigma*) which the Demiurge uses to make the visible world is eternal (*aionios*) and truly perpetual (*aidios*); the sensible world never passes away and therefore is in a sense *aidios*, and so is *eikon kinetos aionos*, 'a moving image of eternity'.

60. **sui naturam:** *naturam iudicis*, not *iudicii.*

68. **cuncta dinoscit:** *cuncta* implies 'all together', 'all in a body', and *dinoscit* 'to know separately', 'to distinguish', so that *cuncta dinoscit* is an untranslateable phrase to describe the knowledge of God which embraces all things in one timeless instant and yet knows each thing separately.

71. **porro a rebus infimis constituta:** 'set far from the lowest things'; *porro*, rare with verbs of rest anyway, is not used with *a, ab* in CL, though it seems

natural enough.

73. **prospiciat:** combining the senses of 'looking forth'
and 'looking after', as does *providere*. The subjunctive is difficult to account for, unless the *quod* =
'as'('the case being such that..')and there is a vague
generic, consecutive sense. But in later Latin the subjunctive in simple relative and causal clauses became
commoner, e.g. *Bell. Hisp.* 35,1: *quibus rebus
Scipio, quique cum eo essent comites, mirari.*

3. BENEDICT AND GREGORY THE GREAT

It may seem a little odd to include in a book like this, concerned with medieval philosophy, extracts from St. Benedict's *Rule* and the *Magna Moralia* of Pope Gregory I; but both works had much to do with the formation of medieval thought, of the 'medieval mind'. Very many of the writers of the Middle Ages were directly influenced by the *Rule* , either as monks or as pupils of monks: for the *Rule* was and still is read aloud to all in the monastery daily, passage by passage, three times a year. In the first week of January, May and September they would hear the Prologue. Reasons for being in a monastery were many; and there were all sorts of reasons why men became monks. Whatever the initial reason - and it was possibly only in few cases that there was a real vocation to the life: men found themselves monks much as young people now find themselves students, and sometimes the causes were economic or political - whatever the actual reason, the Prologue made plain the right reason, and what the aim was and what the effect should be. It set not only the life of the monk but also the life of man in the context of salvation; and in that context, in the hope of Heaven and under the fear of the Judgement all medieval thought took shape.

The importance of the monasteries in the history of early medieval Europe and in preserving and handing on Latin letters is well known. That those monasteries were from the 10th century mostly Benedictine houses was partly due to the policy and encouragement first of Gregory the Great and then of Charlemagne, but mainly to the qualities of the *Rule* itself. It was a modest rule, 'a little rule for beginners' (ch. 73, 8), which encouraged ordinary men not to dedicate themselves to perfection under a Master but to hope and work for salvation in a community. That community was to be stable, under a Father, an abbot: once a monk of Fulda, always a monk of Fulda, unless the abbot permitted otherwise. Each community was to be self-supporting: the *opus manuum,* the labour of maintaining the house, complemented the *opus Dei,* the prayer and services and devotional reading. Within the monastery, and hence within the individual, the *Rule* should produce order and kindness and humility and peace: *pax* is the Benedictines' motto. All life was to be sanctified, the *opus manuum* being as much a movement towards God as the *opus Dei: laborare est orare*.

The very little that is known of St. Benedict himself is derived from Book II of Gregory the Great's *Dialogues*. He was born at Nursia, educated at Rome, retired from study - *recessit igitur scienter nescius, et sapienter indoctus* - to become a solitary at Subiaco, but then founded a monastery and wrote his *Regula*, dying in his own foundation at Monte Cassino in the middle of the 6th century. Gregory describes him as *vir vitae venerabilis, gratia Benedictus et nomine*.

Pope Gregory I, known as St. Gregory the Great, was born a few years before Benedict died, into a wealthy Roman family, in Justinian's reconquered Italy. In the late 560s Justinian was dead and the Lombards invaded the country. Gregory abandoned his administrative career, sold his property and retired to his own monastery. In 590 he was elected Pope and he died in 604. He is known to English schoolchildren - *non Angli sed angeli* - for his sending Augustine to Kent in 596; he gave his name to the plainchant which emerged from his musical reforms; he wrote much: letters, commentaries, the *Dialogues*, a handbook for parish priests known as the *Liber regulae pastoralis*, and the vast commentary on the book of Job begun in the 580s when he was a papal ambassador (*apocrisarius*) in Constantinople, and finished about the turn of the century, known as the *Magna Moralia*. Our extract is taken from the first book of that work, commentary on Job 1, 1-5; it is the beginning of the third and longest commentary on those verses. The first is 'historical', and Gregory introduces the second thus: *Haec breviter historiam sequendo transcurrimus; nunc ordo expositionis exigit ut exordium repetentes, allegoriarum iam secreta pandamus.* So the second is allegorical, and our extract begins with its last and transitional paragraph, which shows that the last commentary is practical, applying Scripture to our lives. The differing levels are typical of medieval commentaries, and indeed Gregory is typically medieval, in his attitudes to hagiography and to miracles, and to pagan learning and Christian endeavour, and in his political life as head of state combating the Lombard invaders. H.O. Taylor described the Middle Ages as a time when 'the peoples of Western Europe..evolved a spirit..which in the actual looked for the ideal, in the concrete saw the symbol, in the earthly church beheld the heavenly, and in fleshly joys discerned the devil's lures..and over which flamed the terror of darkness and the Judgment Day' (*The Medieval Mind*, I, 13). Benedict and Gregory were two of the makers of that spirit.

BIBLIOGRAPHY

Four books only, from the great number available: *Benedictine Monasticism*, ed. C. Butler, London 1919; and one of the best introductions to the Middle Ages, Jean Leclercq's *The Love of Learning and the Desire for God*, translated by C. Misrahi, Fordham 1961; F. Homes Dudden, *Gregory the Great: His Place in History and Thought*, 2 vols, London 1905; and P. Batiffol, *St Gregory the Great*, translated by J.L. Stoddard, London 1929.

[See also now G.R. Evans, *The Thought of Gregory the Great* , Cambridge 1986]

Benedicti Regula, Prologue, ed. R. Hanslik, CSEL, LXXV, 1960

Obsculta, o fili, praecepta magistri et inclina aurem
cordis tui et admonitionem pii patris libenter excipe et
3   efficaciter comple ut ad eum per oboedientiae laborem
redeas, a quo per inoboedientiae desidiam recesseras.
Ad te ergo nunc mihi sermo dirigitur, quisquis abre-
6   nuntians propriis voluntatibus domino Christo vero
regi militaturus oboedientiae fortissima atque praeclara
arma sumis.
9   Inprimis, ut quidquid agendum inchoas bonum, ab
eo perfici instantissima oratione deposcas, ut, qui nos
iam in filiorum dignatus est numero computare, non
12   debet aliquando de malis actibus nostris contristari. Ita
enim ei omni tempore de bonis suis in nobis paren-
dum est, ut non solum iratus pater suos non aliquando
15   filios exheredet, sed nec ut metuendus dominus irri-
tatus a malis nostris ut nequissimos servos perpetuam
tradat ad poenam, qui eum sequi noluerint ad gloriam.
18   Exurgamus ergo tandem aliquando excitante nos
scriptura ac dicente: *Hora est iam nos de somno
surgere*; et apertis oculis nostris ad deificum lumen
21   adtonitis auribus audiamus divina cotidie clamans
quid nos admonet vox dicens: *Hodie si vocem eius
audieritis, nolite obdurare corda vestra*; et iterum: *Qui
24   habet aures audiendi, audiat, quid spiritus dicat eccle-
siis*. Et quid dicit? *Venite, filii, audite me, timorem
domini docebo vos. Currite, dum lumen vitae habetis,
27   ne tenebrae mortis vos comprehendant.*
Et quaerens dominus in multitudinem populi, cui
haec clamat, operarium suum iterum dicit: *Quis est
30   homo, qui vult vitam et cupit videre dies bonos?* Quod
si tu audiens respondeas:'Ego', dicit tibi deus:'Si vis
habere veram et perpetuam vitam, *prohibe linguam
33   tuam a malo et labia tua ne loquantur dolum; deverte a
malo et fac bonum, inquire pacem et sequere eam*. Et
cum haec feceritis, oculi mei super vos et aures meae
36   ad preces vestras, et antequam me invocetis, dicam
vobis: *Ecce adsum*. Quid dulcius nobis ab hac voce

domini invitantis nos, fratres carissimi? Ecce pietate
39 sua demonstrat nobis dominus viam vitae.
   Succinctis ergo fide vel observantia bonorum
actuum lumbis nostris per ducatum evangelii per-
42 gamus itinera eius, ut mereamur eum, *qui nos vocavit
in regnum suum,* videre. In cuius regni tabernaculo si
volumus habitare, nisi illuc bonis actibus curritur,
45 minime pervenitur. Sed interrogemus cum propheta
dominum dicentes ei: *Domine, quis habitavit in taver-
naculo tuo aut quis requiescit in monte sancto tuo?*
48 Post hanc interrogationem, fratres, audiamus dominum respondentem et ostendentem nobis viam ipsius
tabernaculi dicens:*Qui ingreditur sine macula et opera-
51 tur iustitiam; qui loquitur veritatem in corde suo; qui
non egit dolum in lingua sua; qui non fecit proximo
suo malum; qui opprobrium non accepit adversus
54 proximum suum*; qui malignum diabolum aliqua
suadentem sibi cum ipsa suasione sua a conspectibus
cordis sui respuens deduxit ad nihilum et parvulos
57 cogitatos eius tenuit et adlisit ad Christum; qui timen-
tes dominum de bona observantia sua non se reddunt
elatos, sed ipsa in se bona non a se posse, sed a dom-
60 ino fieri existimantes operantem in se dominum mag-
nificant illud cum propheta dicentes: *Non nobis, domine, non nobis, sed nomini tuo da gloriam,* sicut nec
63 Paulus apostolus de praedicatione sua sibi aliquid in-
putavit dicens: *Gratia dei sum ,id quod sum*; et iterum
ipse dicit: *Qui gloriatur, in domino glorietur.* Unde et
66 dominus in evangelio ait: *Qui audit verba mea haec et
facit ea, similabo eum viro sapienti, qui aedificavit
domum suam super petram; venerunt flumina, flav-
69 erunt venti et inpigerunt in domum illam, et non ceci-
dit, quia fundata erat super petram.* Haec complens
dominus exspectat nos cottidie is suis sanctis monitis
72 factis nos respondere debere. Ideo nobis propter emendationem malorum huius vitae dies ad indutias re-
laxantur dicente apostolo:*An nescis, quia patientia dei
75 ad paenitentiam te adducit?* Nam pius dominus dicit:
Nolo mortem peccatoris, sed convertatur et vivat.
Cum ergo interrogassemus dominum, fratres, de

78 habitatore tavernaculi eius, audivimus habitandi praeceptum; sed si compleamus habitatoris officium. Ergo
praeparanda sunt corda et corpora nostra sanctae prae-
81 ceptorum oboedientiae militanda. Et quod minus habet
in nos natura possibile, rogemus dominum, ut gratiae
suae iuvet nobis adiutorium ministrare. Et si fugien-
84 tes gehennae poenas ad vitam volumus pervenire perpetuam, dum adhuc vacat et in hoc corpore sumus et
haec omnia per hanc lucis vitam vacat implere, curren-
87 dum et agendum est modo, quod in perpetuo nobis
expediat.
Constituenda est ergo nobis dominici scola servitii.
90 In qua institutione nihil asperum, nihil grave nos con-
stituturos speramus. Sed et si quid paululum restric-
tius dictante aequitatis ratione propter emendationem
93 vitiorum vel conservationem caritatis processerit, non
ilico pavore perterritus refugias viam salutis, quae non
est nisi angusto initio incipienda. Processu vero con-
96 versationis et fidei dilatato corde inenarrabili dilec-
tionis dulcedine curritur via mandatorum dei, ut ab
ipsius numquam magisterio discidentes in eius doc-
99 trinam usque ad mortem in monasterio perseverantes
passionibus Christi per patientiam participemur, ut et
regno eius mereamur esse consortes.

Notes

1. **Obsculta:** many texts read *ausculta: ab-, au-, a-* are
    all found in the MSS, and the confusion is as old as
    Varro.
    aurem cordis tui: the phrase is probably from Au-
    gustine *Conf.* 1,5, but it is found in older Christian
    writers such as Ambrose, and the idea is in Tertullian.
3. **oboedientiae:** in a monastic context carries the
    meaning of 'monastic obedience' = 'discipline'.
5. **abrenuntians:** with the dative, as usually; a late,
    mainly Christian word. Cf. the baptismal question,
    abrenuntias diabolo et operibus eius? where *diabolo*
    is dative, as shown by Ambrose, *Hexam.* 1,4,14:
    abrenuntio tibi, diabole, et operibus tuis.

7. **militaturus:** with the dative; with *Veneri* in
Apuleius, *Met.*, and synonymous with *servire* in
Cassiodorus.

10. **perfici..deposcas:** the compound *deposco* used
like the simple verb with the accusative and infinitive.
The subjunctive *ut..deposcas* is jussive: 'may you
entreat'.
ut..non debet aliquando: 'that he might never
have to..'; it is impossible sometimes to separate
result from intention, and *ne* and *ut non* are thoroughly confused in LL. The indicative in such
clauses is rare, but *debet* is 'modal'; cf. *ut..necesse
est* in ch.25 of the *Rule*.

12. **de malis actibus:** *de* ='on account of': cf. L.& S.
s.v. C 5, and in the next line *de bonis suis*. For the *in*
of *de bonis suis in nobis* cf. L.& S. s.v. I C; the
attachment of the prepositional phrase *in nobis* thus
adjectivally is natural enough in late writers.

14. **ut non solum..non aliquando:**'that not only..he
might not ever..':*non aliquando=numquam* is common in the Vulgate and in Christian writers.

18. **Exurgamus:** = *exsurgamus;* sometimes the *s* is
there, sometimes not; cf. *exspectat* in line 71.

19. **scriptura:** used in the sing. and plural = 'Scripture',
'Scriptures' from the Latin NT on (e.g. Mk. 14, 49).
de somno: de = *e*; the meaning of *de* was widened
in late and medieval Latin to include most of the uses
of the Romance preposition (cf. Rom. 13,11).

22. **quid nos admonet:** indicative for subjunctive in
indirect question, as often in late, as in early, Latin.
The *dicens* introducing the direct quotation, acting
much as our inverted commas or *hoti* in NT Greek, is
frequently invariable, as in line 50.The quotation is
from Psalm 95, 7-8.

24. *aures audiendi:* the quotation is a conflation of
Mt. 11,15 or 13,9 (or indeed Mk. 4,9) with Rev. 2,7
etc. The Greek of Mt. and Mk. has *ota akouein* 'ears
to hear'; the construction behind it is probably the
Hebrew 'construct infinitive'. In Latin versions the
gerund is often used, and a halfway house between

the simple *potestas calcandi* 'the ability to walk', and the present case is perhaps *tempus revertendi* in Hebr. 11,15 for the Greek *kairon anakampsai* , 'an opportunity to return'.

25. Ps. 34,11 and John 12,35.

28. in multitudinem populi: *in multitudine* most edd., but the confusion of ablative and accusative after prepositions is common enough in later Latin; cf. *in eius doctrinam* in line 88, where editors (and later scribes) emend to *doctrina*. There are too many examples in the *Rule* (e.g. *sine formidinem* in ch.7 and *sine iussionem* regularly) not to be sure that that was what Benedict wrote.

29. Ps. 34,12.

31. si..respondeas..dicit: the confusion of moods is also commonplace; nor is it unknown in CL: Cic., *Caecil.* 6: *cur Siculi te defensorem habere nolint, etiamsi taceant, satis dicunt; verum non tacent.*

32. Ps. 34,13-14.

35. cf. Ps. 24,15. The omission of the copula (*est* or *sunt*) is a Hebraism.

37. cf. Isaiah 65,24 and 58,9. *quid dulcius..ab hoc voce:* the abl. with the comparative is a true 'from which' abl.: 'longer than A' means 'starting from A, go on a bit further', so the use of *a (ab)* with the comparative is natural enough, and it is found in CL, though it is often 'emended out' by editors. E.g. in Ovid, *Her.* 16, 98: *nec Priamo est a te dignior ulla nurus*, some editors print *ad te*; and in Pliny, *N.H.* 18, 126 *usus praestantior ab iis (* or *ab is)* some prefer *praestantior his*. But the comparative with prepositions is common in LL and is found again in the *Rule*. e.g. *si meliores ab aliis in operibus bonis et humiles inveniamur* ch.2,21.

38. pietate sua: the words *pius, pietas,* seem at first to have denoted one's duty to one's parents or relatives or the gods, and then to have been used of any loving relationship involving obligations, and so all loving-kindness. So it came by the 7th c. to be used of God also to mean 'mercy', or simply loving kindness in general.

40. succinctis..lumbis nostris: 'girding up one's loins' is a Biblical expression, used literally in the OL version of Exodus 12,11(and a number of times in the Vulgate elsewhere) usually with *praecingere*; and metaphorically in the OL of Job 38,3. Benedict's phrase is found in Tert., *adv. Marc. 4, 29, succingere debemus lumbos.* The *vel* between *fide* and *observantia* is, as frequently, 'and' not 'or'. *Observantia :* 'performance' is late, but secular as well as Christian.

42. 1 Thess. 2,12.

45. minime: = *non, nullo modo.* See L.& S. *parvus* adv., C 2 B b. It is common in EL and LL.

46. Ps. 15,1. *habitavit:* the MSS are divided between this and the clearly correct *habitabit* (the Vulgate has *habitabit* and *requiescet*). The confusion between *b* and consonantal *u,* which were no doubt pronounced identically, like modern Spanish *b* , as a bilabial fricative, is so common that it is now impossible to be sure which Benedict wrote. However, the present *requiescit* suggests that he was thinking of it as a perfect.

49. viam ipsius tabernaculi: 'the way to his tabernacle', the genitive being Scriptural, from the Hebrew construct case (almost exactly like the place-names in 'Oxford Street', 'Bath Road'); but cf. Cicero and others' use of *via* in such phrases as *via laudis, via gloriae, via mortis,* and in line 39 *viam vitae.*

50. dicens: despite the correct *respondentem, ostendentem* above, invariable. The use is probably influenced by the Hebrew-Aramaic idiom. The quotation is the continuation of Ps. 15.

55. cum ipsa suasione sua: it is most likely that the *sua* here, despite the proximity of *sibi, sui,* refers to the devil; but it would be possible to construe it as an objective genitive = 'that persuasion of himself'. **conspectibus:** the metaphor is Classical enough, but the plural is very late and almost entirely restricted to Christian writers - it is probably derived from the Hebrew through Scriptural uses.

56. deduxit ad nihilum: Cassiodorus has the same
phrase in his commentary on Ps. 15: 'has reduced
(the devil) to nothing'. This use of *deducere* may be
derived from its use in medicine: 'cure', 'remove'.
parvulos cogitatos: 'has taken his (i.e.the devil's)
new-hatched designs and dashed them on (the rock
of) Christ'. *cogitatos* is normally emended to *cogi-*
tatus, but unnecessarily; the confusion of 2nd and 4th
declensions is common, and there is here the addi-
tional confusion of *cogitata, -orum.*

58. de bona observantia: *de* = 'on account of'; see
note on line 12.

61. Ps. 115,1.

64. 1 Cor. 15,10 and 2 Cor. 10,17.

66. Mt. 7,24-25.

71. is: i.e. *his; monitis* is dative, *factis* ablative. The
nos before *respondere* is redundant and one is
tempted to emend to *factis nostris respondere* but that
type of 'tidying up' has to be resisted.

72. propter emendationem: a late, 'final' (purpose)
use of *propter* first found in Valerius Maximus.

73. huius vitae: best taken with *dies* but possibly to be
taken also with *malorum.*

74. Rom. 2,4.

76. Ezech. 33,11. *convertatur* is presumably passive in
Ezechiel 'that he be turned (from his wickedness) and
live', but by the time of Benedict *convertor* was used
intransitively to mean 'be converted', 'enter a monastery', 'become a monk', so there are overtones here.

78. habitandi praeceptum: 'the lodger's rule'. *sed si*
compleamus must mean 'but oh if we might..',
almost a wish, but it is an odd use of *si*. That many
copyists took it this way is shown by their inserting
the unexpressed apodosis, *erimus heredes regni*
caelorum.

81. militanda: 'to serve': beginning in the early Fathers
with all the ferocity of the fight against the devil,
militare, militia had by Benedict's time become practically synonymous with *servire, servitus,* as Christine Mohrmann has shown (*Etudes sur le latin des*

Chrétiens, II, Rome 1961, 337ff.).

minus: = *non,* like *minime;* cf. note on line 45.

in nos: for *in nobis,* with the confusion of cases already remarked on. Again many scribes have introduced the emendation.

82. **gratiae suae iuveat:** *iuveat* = *iubeat,* with the *b/v* confusion; *gratiae suae* is probably dative (used with *iubere* by Livy and Tacitus and later authors): 'command his grace to provide help for us'.

86. **hanc lucis vitam:** *lucis* here probably means 'the world'; classification of the genitive is a grammarian's game - sort, material, quality, description, - or place? It clearly means 'this life in the world'.

87. **modo, quod in perpetuo:** *modo* = 'now'; *quod* = *id quod; in perpetuo* confuses *in perpetuum* and *perpetuo.*

92. **dictante ratione:** not so much absolute as ablative of cause: *ratio aequitatis* almost = 'right or fair reason'.

93. **caritatis:** in its widest sense of Christian love, Christian life.
    non ilico..refugias: *non* with the subjunctive in place of the strictly correct *ne,* for prohibitions, is so common in LL as almost to be the rule; so that *non confundar in aeternum* at the end of the *Te Deum* is surely rightly translated 'let me never be confounded', not as a future.

95. **conversationis:** 'the religious life' = the life of a monk. There is an excellent note on this word in Abbot Justin McCann's edition of the *Rule,* London 1952, on pp.168 and 202ff. His conclusion is that it has two basic meanings : active = *introitus in vitam monachorum,* practically = *conversio* ; and middle = *vita ac consuetudo monachi,* as in our passage. It might be worth adding that *conversatio* is used to mean 'frequent abode in a place' by Pliny and in the *Digest.*

98. **in eius doctrinam:** accusative for ablative again.

99. **monasterio:** the Greek word is derived from *monos* 'alone'; and a *monachos,* a monk, was originally a

man living alone in the desert (a hermit, from *eremos* = 'desert', or an anchorite, *anachoites*, one who went up into the country, from *anachorein*). *Monasterium* meant 1) 'a hermit's cell'; 2) 'a house for a few *monachi* '; and finally 3) 'a monastery'. All three meanings are found in the late 4th-c. Aetheria's account of her journey to Jerusalem, and in the works of Jerome,her younger and greater contemporary.

Sancti Gregorii Magni Moralia in Iob 1,33-38 ed.
M. Adriaen, CCSL CXLIII, Turnhout 1979.

Igitur quia in ipso expositionis exordio sic persona
beati Iob nuntiari Dominum diximus ut designari per
3   illum caput et corpus, id est Christum et Ecclesiam
diceremus, postquam caput nostrum quomodo desig-
natum credatur ostendimus, nunc corpus eius, quod
6   nos sumus, quomodo exprimatur, indicemus, ut quia
audivimus ex historia quod miremur, cognovimus ex
capite quod credamus, consideremus nunc ex corpore
9   quod vivendo teneamus. In nobismetipsis namque
debemus transformare quod legimus, ut cum per
auditum se animus excitat, ad operandum quod
12   audierit vita concurrat.
    Vir erat in terra Hus nomine Iob. Si Iob dolens et
Hus consiliator dicitur, non immerito per utraque
15   nomina electus quisque figuratur, quia nimirum con-
siliatorem animum inhabitat, quia dolens de praesentibus ad aeterna festinat. Nam sunt nonnulli qui vitam
18   suam negligunt et dum transitoria appetunt, dum
aeterna vel non intellegunt, vel intellecta contemnunt,
nec dolorem sentiunt, nec habere consilium sciunt.
21   Cumque superna, quae amiserunt, non considerant,
esse se, heu miseri, in bonis putant. Nequaquam enim
ad veritatis lucem, cui conditi fuerant, mentis oculos
24   erigunt; nequaquam ad contemplationem aeternae
patriae desiderii aciem tendunt sed semetipsos in his
quo proiecti sunt deserentes, vice patriae diligunt
27   exsilium quod patiuntur et in caecitate, quam tolerant,
quasi in claritate luminis exsultant. At contra electorum mentes dum cuncta transitoria nulla esse conspic-
30   iunt, ad quam sint conditae exquirunt. Cumque eorum
satisfactioni nil extra Deum sufficit, ipsa inquisitionis
exercitatione fatigata illorum cogitatio, in conditoris
33   sui spe et contemplatione requiescit, supernis interseri
civibus appetit. Et unusquisque eorum adhuc in mundo corpore positus, mente iam extra mundum surgit,
36   aerumnam exsilii quam tolerat, deplorat et ad sublimem patriam incessantibus se amoris stimulis excitat.

Cum ergo dolens videt quam sit aeternum quod per-
39   didit, invenit salubre consilium, temporale hoc des-
picere quod percurrit; et quo magis crescit consilii
scientia ut peritura deserat, eo augetur dolor, quod
42   necdum ad mansura pertingat. Unde bene per Salo-
monem dicitur: *Qui apponit scientiam, apponit dolorem.* Qui enim scit iam summa quae adhuc non habet,
45   magis de infimis in quibus retinetur dolet.

Recte ergo in terra Hus habitare Iob dicitur quia in
scientiae consilio electi uniuscuiusque dolens animus
48   tenetur. Intuendum quoque est quam nullus dolor
mentis sit in actione praecipitationis. Qui enim sine
consiliis vivunt, qui ipsos se rerum eventibus   prae-
51   cipites deserunt, nullo interim cogitationum dolore
fatigantur. Nam qui solerter in vitae consilio figit
mentem, caute sese in omni actione circumspiciendo
54   considerat. Et ne ex re quae agitur repentinus finis
adversusque subripiat, hunc prius molliter posito
pede cogitationis palpat, pensat ne ab his quae agenda
57   sunt formido praepediat; ne in his quae differenda
sunt praecipitatio impellat; ne prava per concupiscentiam aperto bello superent; ne recta per inanem
60   gloriam insidiando supplantent. Iob ergo in terra Hus
habitat, dum mens electi quo magis per consilium
vivere nititur, eo angusti itineris dolore fatigatur.
63   Sequitur: *Simplex et rectus, timens Deum et recedens a malo.* Quisquis aeternam patriam appetit, simplex procul dubio et rectus vivit; simplex videlicet
66   opere, rectus fide; simplex in bonis quae inferius
peragit, rectus in summis quae in intimis sentit. Sunt
namque nonnulli qui in bonis quae faciunt simplices
69   non sunt, dum non in his retributionem interius sed
exterius favorem quaerunt. Unde bene per quemdam
sapientem dicitur: *Vae peccatori terram ingredienti
72   duabus viis.* Duabus quippe viis peccator terram
ingreditur quando et Dei est quod opere exhibet et
mundi quod per cogitationem quaerit.
75   Bene autem dicitur: *Timens Deum et recedens a
malo*, quia sancta electorum Ecclesia simplicitatis suae

et rectitudinis vias timore inchoat, sed caritate con-
78 summat. Cui tunc est funditus a malo recedere cum ex
amore Dei coeperit iam nolle peccare. Cum vero
adhuc timore bona agit, a malo penitus non recessit,
81 quia eo ipso peccat, quo peccare vellet si inulte potu-
isset. Recte ergo cum timere Deum Iob dicitur, recedere etiam a malo perhibetur, quia dum metum caritas
84 sequitur, ea quae mente relinquitur, etiam per
cogitationis propositum culpa calcatur.
     Et quia ex timore unumquodque vitium premitur,
87 ex caritate autem virtutes oriuntur, recte subiungitur:
Natique sunt ei septem filii et tres filiae. Septem
quippe nobis filii nascuntur cum per conceptionem
90 bonae cogitationis, sancti Spiritus septem in nobis
virtutes oriuntur. Hanc namque internam prolem
propheta dinumerat, cum Spiritus mentem fecundat,
93 dicens: *Requiescet super eum Spiritus Domini,*
spiritus sapientiae et intellectus, spiritus consilii et for-
titudinis, spiritus scientiae et pietatis; et replebit eum
96 *spiritus timoris Domini.* Cum ergo per adventum
Spiritus, sapientia, intellectus, consilium, fortitudo,
scientia, pietas ac timor Domini unicuique nostrum
99 gignitur, quasi mansura posteritatis in mente propa-
gatur quae supernae nostrae nobilitatis genus eo ad
vitam longius servat, quo amori aeternitatis sociat.
102 Sed habent in nobis septem filii tres procul dubio
sorores suas quia quicquid virile hi virtutum sensus
faciunt, spei, fidei caritatique coniungunt. Neque
105 enim ad denarii perfectionem septem filii perveniunt
nisi in spe, fide et caritate fuerit omne quod agunt.

Notes

1. The punctuation of this first paragraph has been
    changed from that of Adriaen, which obscures the
    meaning.
    persona: ablative.
2. **Iob:** genitive - most Hebrew names being indec-
    linable in Latin.
7. **ex historia..ex capite:** i.e. from the first and

second commentaries.

quod miremur..: the confusions in the use of
quod/quid in questions, direct and indirect, even in
CL, are evident from the tergiversations of grammarians trying to explain them, since they feel that
language must follow some sorts of rules. If one
needs grammarians' jargon for this one can say that
the *quod* in each case is 'that which', and the subjunctives are a kind of jussive - 'we ought to'. Cf.
quod legimus in line 10 - 'that which we read'.

9. **in nobismetipsis..transformare:** the ablative
   means 'in our very selves', and *transformare* is
   literally 'transform', 'change', i.e. 'assimilate'.

11. **quod audierit vita:** *audierit* fut. perf. 'that which
    it has (shall have) heard'; *vita* is ablative, the subject
    still being *animus* 'the mind': 'so that when the mind
    is stirred up by what it has heard, it should go along
    with it in living to do what it has heard'. *Concurrere*
    is used here in a sense closer to the English 'concur'
    than anything cited in L.& S., though Tertullian has it
    (see TLL) in a literal 'go along with' sense.

13. The translations *dolens* for the Hebrew *Iob*, and
    consiliator for *Hus*, made much of in the previous
    commentary, are from Jerome's book on Hebrew
    names, the great standby of medieval interpreters.

15. **electus:** in the Scriptural sense of 'chosen'.
    figuratur: it seems this metaphorical use did not
    develop before the Christian writers needed it.

16. **de praesentibus:** it is impossible to say whether it
    is *dolens de praesentibus* or *de praesentibus ad*
    aeterna; de will bear either interpretation. Perhaps
    both are intended?

23. **conditi fuerant:** 'they were created' - aorist
    passive.

30. **ad quam sint conditae:** Adriaen changed MSS'
    quem to *quam* (referring to *veritatis lux* above) but
    surely unnecessarily: *quem* would be God, as the
    following *nil extra Deum* indicates. *Sint conditae* is
    indirect question: 'they seek to find for whom they
    have been made'.

cumque..sufficit: in line 21 *cumque..non considerant* may be construed as 'at the same time as':
what Roby's *Latin Grammar* described as 'a contrast
of actions' is sometimes done with the indicative -
probably more in colloquial Latin, since Cicero does it
more often in his letters than in his speeches. It is
really, perhaps, an extension of the 'coincidence in
time, especially when combined with an identity of
person and tense' (Roby). So here one may translate
cumque as 'and although' or 'and at the same time
as'.

33. **interseri:** apart from Ovid's *oscula mediis verbis*
from *Met.* 10,519, the earliest metaphorical uses of
this verb are 3rd c.

39. **salubre:** there is the sense of 'saving', 'salvation',
from *salus*, cf. Macc. 12,46: *sancta et salubris est
cogitatio pro defunctis exorare.*

43. *Qui apponit:* Eccles. 1,18. *apponit* = 'increases'.
Strictly, perhaps, one should say 'add *scientiam sibi*
or *suae scientiae'*, but from 'adds' to 'increases' is a
small step.

48. **quam:** 'how'; see L.& S. s.v. init.

49. **in actione praecipitationis:** a phrase which,
while consisting of entirely CL words, is purely ML
in feel; its Biblical genitive is derived partly from CL
uses such as *actio gratiarum* and partly from the
Hebrew-Aramaic construct case.

53. **sese..circumspiciendo considerat:** this metaphorical use of *considerare* as a reflexive verb,
though seemingly natural enough, is not earlier than
Seneca.

55. **subripiat, hunc:** the punctuation must be wrong
here: *hunc* is the object of transitive *subripiat; palpat,
pensat* revert to the same subject, *qui solerter* etc.;
'lest..an unforeseen and adverse end should steal him
away (lead him astray)' - 'his thought steps gently at
first and he feels his way, pondering so that caution
does not trip him and keep him from what he has to
do'. For *palpare* = to feel the way like a blind man,
see Job 5,14. It is impossible to say whether *ex re*

quae agitur means 'out of the matter in hand' with *finis*, or 'on account of' or 'from..' with *subripiat*.

59. ne recta..supplantent: the verb is intransitive here, as occasionally in the Vulgate, e.g. Jerem. 9,4.

61. dum mens electi: *dum* here = 'while'= 'since', as occasionally in CL; a use illustrated in most grammar books but not in L.& S. There is in LL much confusion between *cum* and *dum* with the indicative and subjunctive, but not here in Gregory. Cf. *dum..quaerunt* in line 69.

62. angusti itineris: metaphorically, from Biblical usage, e.g. Mt. 7,14: *angusta porta et arta via*.

69. retributionem: 'repayment'; a Christian word, used both in a good and bad sense in the early Fathers.

70. per quemdam sapientem: Eccles. 2.14.

88. *septem filii et tres filiae:* numbers in the sacred text invited commentary, of course. Where all is inspired, all is significant. Why seven and three? Why not six and four? So numbers give ample scope for allegorical interpretation, amply used by Gregory. Seven is, of course, a special number: there are seven deadly sins - a list possibly derived from the Stoics and found in Horace, *Ep.* 1,1,33ff. - seven gifts or virtues of the Holy Spirit (cf. Ambrose, *Ep.* 31,3), the seven seals and seven trumpets for the seven churches in the Apocalypse, and 'seven stars in the sky' (i.e. sun, moon and visible planets. Three is not only the Trinity, but the number of the theological virtues - faith, hope and charity; and so on. Those interested might consult: T. Zielinski in *Philologus* LXIV,1905, 21ff; H. Meyer, *Die Zahlenallegorese im Mittelalter: Methode und Gebrauch,* Munchen 1975; Klibansky, Panofsky and Saxl, *Saturn and Melancholy,* London 1964, pp.159ff; and also, though it is a bit of an *omnium gatherum,* V.F. Hooper, *Medieval Number Symbolism,* Columbia 1938.

92. propheta..dicens: Isaiah 11,2-3.

99. mansura: 'enduring', 'permanent'; cf. Virg. *Aen.*3,86, which is possibly where Gregory got it .

100 genus: probably more like 'kinship' here; cf.
Boethius, *Porph.Isag,* p.26,2 on *genus.*

105 ad denarii perfectionem: 'to the perfection of
ten', i.e. seven plus three. Ten's perfection derives
ultimately from the Pythagoreans.

4. JOHN SCOTUS ERIGENA

Erigena is surely the most extraordinary figure in the story of early medieval thought, extraordinary being used in a literal sense of one who by the strength and originality of his mind stood out head and shoulders above all other thinkers of the period; added to which he was a layman, which makes him almost unique among medieval scholars.

In the centuries between Boethius and Bede the Classical culture had all but disappeared on the continent of Europe. Only in two places, in Italy and in Ireland, were there centres of learning. These two traditions, the Italian and the Irish, flowed together in the twin monasteries of St. Peter and St. Paul founded by Benedict Biscop in Northumberland, to produce in the 7th century the lamp of Anglo-Saxon learning, one of the great and humble men of the Middle Ages, Bede the Venerable, historian, teacher, scholar and saint. It was a pupil of Bede, Egbert, who taught in the cathedral school of York the man who directed the educational reforms of Charlemagne, Alcuin. From the school of Alcuin, Peter of Pisa and Paul the Deacon, there is a direct tradition of learning in the Empire, through Rabanus Maurus under Louis the Pious to the circle of 9th-century savants under Charles the Bald: Ratramn of Corbie, Lupus of Ferrières (an attractive figure, with his passion for books and his accurate scholarship), Hincmar the Bishop of Rheims, Sedulius Scottus, Walafrid Strabo with his garden, Godescalc of Orbais, and Erigena.

It was an age of religious controversy, concerned mainly with two problems, the nature of the Eucharist and Predestination. Godescalc (or Gottschalk, 'Theodoulos': 'the slave of God') produced, not for the first nor the last time in the history of the Church, the theory of God's predestination not only of the good to salvation, but of the wicked to eternal damnation. In 850 Erigena was asked by Bishop Pardulus of Laon to refute the errors of the monk of Orbais. That he should have been asked to engage in so important a controversy argues that his reputation was already considerable and well-established. He had been at the court of Charles for three or four years. Of his life practically nothing is known. His name was spelt Johannes Scotus (or Scottus) Erigena (or better, Eriugena); *Scot(t)us* before the 11th c. meant 'Irish', and *Eriugena* presumably means 'born of Erin', though there is some doubt that it really ever was part of his name. The spelling *Erigena*, now standard, is first found in a 13th-c. MS. He was born in Ireland some time early in the 9th c., but we do not know how much of his learning, and in particular his exceptional knowledge of Greek, he acquired in Ireland. Did he learn his Greek on the continent (if so, where?), or in the Irish schools before they were ravaged by the Norse invasions? He was neither monk nor cleric, probably taught at the Palace school, and died some time after 870, we do not know where. Of his work in rhetoric and grammar little is known, but the influence of his teaching is seen in the next generation, in the writings of Heiric and Rémy of Auxerre. Apart from his *Liber de Praedestinatione*, which was unorthodox enough in its methods and conclusions to get its author into trouble with ecclesiastical authority, Erigena is best known for his construction in the *De Divisione Naturae* of a full-blown Neoplatonic system of philosophy and theology, based on the works he himself had translated from the Greek of 'Dionysius the Areopagite'.

These works were 5th-c. forgeries which claimed as their author St. Paul's only Athenian convert (Acts 17,34); which Dionysius, or Denis, was later identified with the Apostle of Gaul. The falsity of this latter identification was shown by Abelard among others, to the discomfiture and annoyance of the monks of St. Denis, but the genuineness of the Dionysian authorship of the treatises bearing the Areopagite's name was not seriously questioned before Thomas Aquinas, who however still made great use of them. These treatises, on the Celestial and Ecclesiastical Hierarchies, on Mystical Theology, and on the Divine Names, owed much to the Neoplatonist Proclus, and Erigena's system, derived from them, was sufficiently Neoplatonist to bring upon him accusations of being a pantheist and a gnostic. We are here, however, concerned only with two points: the negative theology and the problem of evil.

Erigena found the distinction between positive (or affirmative) and negative theology in the works of the Pseudo-Dionysius and of Maximus the Confessor, who wrote *Ambigua*, a discussion of some difficulties in the Greek theologians. The negative theology consists in saying not that God is this or that, but simply that he is not this or that - infinite, ineffable, and so on - so that he is better known in not-knowing (i.e. knowing what he is not, not not-knowing what he is) than in knowing. It is based on and arises out of the difficulty of applying human terms (which are all we have) to God; a problem which recurs again and again in medieval philosophy. Our language is fashioned for human things; how then in this language can we say anything about a transcendent God? If a Christian says, 'Socrates is' and then 'God is', the word 'is' is used in two different senses, since in the first case if existence is predicated it is contingent, and in the second it is necessary. One's answer to this problem is intimately bound up with one's views on equivocation and analogy; which is why an apparently dry-as-dust treatise *On Equivocation* may be of living importance to the theologian, and why one should not be over-eager to condemn the 'logic-chopping' of the schools. Indeed, the logicians of the 14th c., and especially perhaps Ockham, were much concerned with the problems of analogy and equivocation, and the predication of anything of God.

The very existence of evil in the world is a long-standing problem, since everything that is was made by God and all that he made is good. The traditional answer (from Plato ultimately, via Neo-platonism), Augustine's answer, was that evil does not really exist at all, being only the privation of good, having itself no proper essence. This does not, of course, explain the origin of evil, but only disposes of its 'existence' in the world. The question of the freedom of man, free will, which is at the root of the problem of the origin of evil, will arise later in these extracts. It was not in his denial of true existence to evil that Erigena was unorthodox, but in his ideas on the end of the world - *quando.. universaliter est peritura malitia* (1 Cor. 15,20-28; what St. Paul meant by this extraordinary passage is very far from clear, and is too large a subject for here, as well as being not entirely relevant). Erigena's ideas on the total disappearance of evil, expressed in the *Liber de Praedestinatione* in 851, were condemned at the Synod of Valence in 855 and again at Langres in 859. In Book V of the *De Divisione Naturae*, written some 10 years after Langres, he saves the eternity of the punishment of the damned in an ingenious but not wholly convincing way, involving the 'reality' of *phantasiae rerum temporalium*. That is however a strictly theological problem and not a philosophical one, but the problem of evil has philosophical, ethical implications, and in Christian ethics especially it is difficult if not impossible to separate philosophy from theology.

The second extract is from his commentary on the *De Nuptiis Mercurii et Philologiae* of Martianus Capella, a 5th-c. encyclopaedia of the liberal arts. This curious work, written partly in prose and partly in verse (a form known as 'Menippean Satire') is the account of the wedding, before all the assembled gods, of the lady Philologia to the god Mercury. Philology has been given seven sisters as bridesmaids, and as each in turn introduces herself to the company she explains what she does. The first is Grammatica, the second Rhetorica, the third Dialectica, and so on, so that Books III to IX are a summary encyclopaedia of the seven liberal arts, at a very elementary level, but nevertheless one of the more 'advanced' textbooks of the early Middle Ages. Our extract serves not only to introduce Martianus Capella, but also the genre, the commentary. Much medieval philosophical and theological thought is enshrined in commentaries, on Scripture, on the Fathers, on any *auctoritas*. Medieval scholars pinned even their original speculations on to some older, or even contemporary source or 'authority' - even when they were so 'interpreting' their *auctoritas* as to contradict him! We shall later come across one of the most important kinds of commentary (on the *Sentences* of Peter Lombard), but commentaries on Martianus, as on the Neoplatonist Macrobius' work, itself a commentary on the *Dream of Scipio* from the end of Cicero's *De Re Publica*, enabled a scholar to air his knowledge of and his speculations on the subjects of the quadrivium, especially arithmetic (numbers) and astronomy. It was in these commentaries on late antique encyclopaedic works that much of the scientific knowledge of the ancients was handed on to the Middle Ages. Our extract continues the kind of thinking we have just seen in Gregory the Great - the interpretation of numbers and the kind of 'number theory' found in what was called arithmetic.

It is difficult to estimate the influence of Erigena on later thought. His translations of Pseudo-Dionysius etc. were later replaced by better ones, such as Hilduin's in the 11th c., but there was certainly some influence on the mystical school of St. Victor in Paris, and possibly on later mystics. A recent example of his influence - non-philosophical - is in the work of Ezra Pound. But he remains interesting simply in and for himself, a sort of super-nova among the distant stars of the Carolingian renaissance.

BIBLIOGRAPHY

The best books in English are *John Scotus Erigena*, by H. Bett, Cambridge 1925, and the chapter in R.L. Poole's *Illustrations of the History of Medieval Thought*, London 1884; but the standard work is Dom M. Cappuyns, *Jean Scot Erigène: sa vie, son oeuvre, sa pensée,*

Louvain 1933. The latest contribution to studies on Erigena is a collection of over 40 essays from a conference held at Laon in 1975: *Jean Scot Erigène et l'histoire de la philosophie*, Paris 1977. There is a partial translation, with summaries of the omitted portions, of the *Periphyseon* by M.L. Uhlfelder, Indianapolis 1976.

1. Erigena: Negative Theology; Evil
De Divisione Naturae 1,66 ed. I.P. Sheldon-Williams,
Scriptores Latini Hiberniae VII, Dublin 1968

Ratio vero in hoc universaliter studet ut suadeat
certisque veritatis investigationibus approbet nil de
3   Deo proprie posse dici quoniam superat omnem intellectum omnesque sensibiles intelligibilesque signifi-
cationes qui melius nesciendo scitur, cuius ignorantia
6   vera est sapientia, qui verius fideliusque negatur in
omnibus quam firmatur. Quodcunque enim de ipso
negaveris vere negabis, non autem omne quodcunque
9   firmaveris vere firmabis. Siquidem si approbaveris
hoc vel hoc illum esse falsitatis redargueris, quia
omnium quae sunt quae dici vel intelligi possunt nihil
12   est; si vero pronuntiaveris: 'Nec hoc nec illud nec
ullum ille est', verax esse videberis, quia nihil horum
quae sunt et quae non sunt est, ad quem nemo potest
15   accedere nisi prius corroborato mentis itinere sensus
omnes deserat et intellectuales operationes et sensibilia
et omne quod est et quod non est et ad unitatem (ut
18   possibile est) inscius restituatur ipsius qui est super
omnem essentiam et intelligentiam, cuius neque ratio
est neque intelligentia neque dicitur neque intelligitur
21   neque nomen eius est neque verbum. Non autem irrationabiliter, ut saepe diximus, omnia quae a summo
usque deorsum sunt de eo dici possunt quadam simi-
24   litudine aut dissimilitudine aut contrarietate aut oppo-
sitione quoniam ab ipso omnia sunt quae de eo praedicari possunt. Non enim similia sibi solummodo
27   condidit sed etiam dissimilia quoniam ipse similis est
et dissimilis, contrariorum quoque causa est. Virtute
siquidem eorum quae vere ab eo condita sunt ea etiam
30   quae contraria videntur esse et per privationem essentiae non sunt vera ratio contineri approbat. Nullum
enim vitium invenitur quod non sit alicuius virtutis
33   umbra aut quadam fallaci similitudine aut aperta contrarietate: similitudine quidem ut superbia verae poten-
tiae umbram gerit, luxuria quietis, furor fortitudinis,
36   ira correctionis iustitiaeque et similia; contrarietate

vero ut malitia bonitatis. Quemadmodum enim bonitas
ex non existentibus existentia ducit ut sint, ita malitia
39   appetit corrumpere omnia quae sunt et penitus solvere
ne sint, et si hoc esset id est si omnia perirent simul et
ipsa periret. Nam si periret natura periret simul et
42   vitium. Sed virtute bonitatis omnis natura continetur
ne pereat. Adhuc tamen malitia permittitur in ea videlicet natura ad laudem bonitatis ex contraria compara-
45   tione et exercitationem virtutum rationabili operatione
et purgationem ipsius naturae quando absorbebitur
mors in victoria et sola bonitas in omnibus et appare-
48   bit et regnabit et universaliter peritura malitia. Sed de
his in quinto latius disputabitur. Nulla itaque auctoritas te terreat ab his quae rectae contemplationis ratio-
51   nabilis suasio edocet. Vera enim auctoritas rectae
rationi non obsistit, neque recta ratio verae auctoritati.
Ambo siquidem ex uno fonte, divina videlicet sapien-
54   tia, manare dubium non est.

Notes

1.   **universaliter:** 'generally'; in a literal sense, now
uncommon, meaning 'in all cases'.
3.   **superat:** if this verb is regarded as sub-oblique after
suadeat..nil posse dici, it ought to be in the subjunctive; but it possibly expresses the cause, rather, of
reason's persuading us etc.
sensibiles: 'sensible' in the philosophical sense,
'perceivable by the senses', opposed to *intelligibiles*,
'perceivable by the mind', thus eliminating all meanings having relevance to human powers of knowing.
5.   **qui melius:** cf. Ps.Dion., *De Cael Hier*. II,3: '
'Sometimes it (the divine essence) is named by these
same Scriptures in a supernatural way by dissimilar
qualities - calling it invisible (1 Tim. 6,16) and infinite
(Ps. 144,13) and ineffable (Rom. 11,33) and other
names from among those signifying not what it is but
what it is not; and this, I believe, is more proper to it'.
Cf. also *De Myst. Theol.* I,2: 'when they ought to
affirm of it all the statements about created things, as
being the cause of them all, and more properly deny

them all of it, as surpassing all things'.

cuius ignorantia: cf. 1 Cor. 1,21-25, esp. *quia quod stultum est Dei, sapientius est hominibus.* St. Paul's implication is that the 'ignorance' of God (subjective genitive) is wiser than man's wisdom. The context here points to an objective genitive, *cuius*, not 'whose ignorance', but 'ignorance of whom'.

9. **siquidem si:** 'since indeed if'; *siquidem = quandoquidem* occasionally in CL (see L.&.S. s.v. *siquidem* II) and cf. lines 29, 53 below. *Siquidem si* is thus a natural collocation of particles, though rare.

10. **falsitatis redargueris:** the genitive of the fault is found in CL with the simple verb *arguere*, but not with the compound *redarguere*, before Lactantius.

11. **dici:** 'be spoken of' = expressed in words, and so = described; cf. Vell. Paterc. II,13: *vir neque silendus neque dicendus sine cura.*

14. **quae sunt et quae non sunt:** expressing the Greek *ta onta kai ouk onta.* See next note.

15. **nisi prius..:** a difficult sentence whose meaning is clarified by comparison with its source: *ipsius* (line 18) refers to God and is to be taken with *ad unitatem*; cf. Ps.Dion. *De Myst. Theol.* I,1: 'Do you, my dear Timothy, in the earnest and intent practice of mystic contemplation, leave behind the senses and intellectual activities, and all sensible and intelligible things, and all things that are and are not, and as is possible, be lifted up, not knowing how, to union with him who is above all being and knowing'. Cf. Erigena's translation of this passage: *tu autem, O amice Timothee, circa mystica speculationes corroborato itinere et sensus desere et intellectuales operationes et sensibilia et invisibilia et omne non ens et ens; et ad unitatem, ut possibile, inscius restituere* (=passive imperative) *ipsius qui est super omnem essentiam et scientiam.* Notice how when translating from the Greek Erigena uses *non ens et ens*, whereas in his original writing he uses *quae sunt et quae non sunt*, which strikingly recalls the practice of Boethius, who in translations of and commentaries on the Greek logical works uses

ens, but in his theological tractates and in the *Conso-latio* always uses *quod est*. See E. Gilson in *Medieval Studies*, 8,1946, pp.150ff. for notes on *ens, essentia, existentia. Ens, entis*, that present participle of *sum*, so much desired by elementary prose-writers, accor-ding to Quintilian was made up by a Flavius or Fabi-anus, and according to Priscian first used by Caesar (though not in his extant works); it only became common in the philosophers after Boethius.

17. unitatem: = the act of becoming one with; *unitas*, like *unio*, which Jerome used when faced with the same problem (*Ep.*22,19: *Maria Dei unione fecunda*) usually refers to the result, the unity or oneness.

19. ratio: used here like the Greek *logos*, to mean 'account', a rational description; it is rarely so used in CL, though many instances come close to it, e.g. Plaut., *Poen. prol. 55:nomen iam habetis, nunc rationes ceteras accipe* = 'a description of the rest'.

20. dicitur: see note on line 11.

23. usque deorsum: 'right down' to the lowest; in CL the normal phrase is *ab imo ad summum* or vice-versa: *usque deorsum* does not occur. However, *usque* is often used with adverbs, as *usque istinc, usque adhuc*, both from Cicero.

25. praedicari: used by Boethius and Cassiodorus to translate the Greek *katêgorein*, 'to predicate' = to attribute something to something else in a proposition 'A is..'. Thus Aristotle's *Categories* is an account of the different kinds of predicates there are. As to attri-buting the predicates of the *Categories* to God, cf. *De Div. Nat.* 1,14: *de conditore rerum per metaphoram, significandi gratia, dicuntur*.

30. per privationem essentiae non sunt: because they have no substance, no essence or proper exis-tence. Note how when to this principle is added that *malitia* is contrary to *bonitas*, it follows that evil does not properly speaking exist.

31. contineri: 'kept in existence', cf. line 42. *Continere* in CL is used to mean 'preserve','hold together', e.g. Cic. *De Off. II,24,84: nec ulla res vehementius rem*

publicam continet quam fides; cf. also the Vulgate,
*Sap.*1,7: *quoniam spiritus Domini replevit orbem
terrarum, et hoc, quod continet omnia, scientiam
habet vocis.*

38. existentibus: substantivally, 'existents, things that
exist'.

39. appetit corrumpere: for the use of *appetere* with
an infinitive as object, 'to grasp at', cf. Cic. *De Fin.
V,20,55: ut appetat animus agere semper aliquid.*

43. adhuc: probably temporally, 'as yet' - until the end
of the world.
permittitur: always with the dative in CL and so
only impersonally in the passive. There is one doubtful passive in Seneca and it does occur in inscriptions; cf. also Boethius, *De Cath. Fide* 142: *et qui
numerosam annorum seriem permissus fuerat vivere.*

46. absorbebitur: cf. I Cor. 15,54: *cum autem mortale
hoc induerit immortalitatem, tunc fiet sermo qui scrip-
tus est: absorpta est mors in victoria.* Cf. also II Cor.
5,4.

49. nulla..terreat: possibly potential subjunctive, but
much more likely jussive, with *nulla = ne ulla.*

51. vera enim auctoritas: although this is the orthodox view of the relation between reason and authority, Erigena inclined to a rather unorthodox ratio-
nalism. He never questioned the authority of the
Scriptures, *verissima auctoritas,* but all other 'authorities' were human, and therefore based on, and so
inferior to, reason: *omnis auctoritas quae vera ratione
non approbatur, infirma videtur esse (De Div. Nat.*I,
69). This did not, however, prevent Erigena from
quoting the usual authorities, esp. Augustine, in his
own support.

54. manare dubium non est: the accusative and infinitive is found with *dubium est* in Terence and Livy,
but the negative *dubium non est* would have required
quin with the subjunctive in CL.

2. Erigena: Numbers
Annotationes in Marcianum, ed. C. Lutz, Cambridge (Mass.) 1939

EPTAS in numeris Septenarius numerus tribuitur
Palladi multis modis: primo modo quia omnes numeri
3   qui sunt intra denarium numerum aut generant aut ge-
nerantur, septenarius vero nec generat nec generatur,
quia per nullius numeri duplicationem generatur nec
6   generat aliquem numerum infra denarium per duplicationem. Verbi gratia, duo duplicati pariunt IIII, tria
<a> nullo duplicato nascuntur, ipsa duplicata pariunt
9   senarium; quattuor numerus et parit et paritur, paritur
autem ab bis duobus, parit autem duplicatus octona-
rium; quinque numerus a nullo nascitur bis supputato,
12   ipse bis supputatus parit decem. Item sex numerus
nascitur quidem ex duplicata triade, parit autem infra
decimum limitem neminem; octavus nascitur ex bis
15   supputatis quattuor, ipse neminem parit; nonus nascitur ex ter tribus, ipse neminem parit. Decimus nascitur
ex duplicato numero, ipse porro neminem parit. Atque
18   omnibus partim nascentibus, partim parientibus, partim et nascentibus et parientibus, solus septenarius
numerus neque ex duplicatione alterius nascitur nec
21   infra decimum limitem parit quemquam, propterea
Minervae datur. Minerva dicitur quasi *Minerva; min*
non, *erva* mortalis, igitur Minerva inmortalis dicitur.
24   Alio modo septenarius tribuitur Minervae quia multa
eorum quae naturae lege proveniunt iuxta hunc numerum fieri notantur. Principio septimani partus ante
27   caeteros legitimi sunt in generis humani fetibus, id est
qui fiunt in septimo mense, deinde quod post partus
septimo mense dentes aguntur, septimo deinceps anno
30   mutantur. Post idem septimus annus affert utrique
sexui gignendique et pariendi maturitatem; inde septimo anno ostendit se flos et lanugo circa genas. Item
33   inde septimo finiuntur more mentis staturae; item inde
septimo iuvenilis aetas affert perfectionem, sic semper
per septenarium numerum usque in decrepitum vadit.
36   Iterum septem meatus sunt in capite, oculorum aurium

narium atque oris. Vitalia quoque membra sunt
septem: lingua pulmo cor lien epar duo renes. Nume-
39   rus quoque vocalium litterarum Graecarum septenarius est, id est quinque vocales antiquae et *a* producta
et *o* producta. Luna quoque crescentis et senescentis
42   septem formas habet, siquidem de obscura crescente
luminis sit bicornis, dehinc sectilis, dehinc dimidiato
maior, dehinc plena; sic in decrescendo maior dimi-
45   diato, sectilis, bicornis. Septem quoque planete sunt
in mundo. Musica item caelestis septem spatia habet et
septem tonos. Item septenarius intra se continet totam
48   rationabilem creaturam, id est hominem. Habet enim
septenarius intra se ternarium et quaternarium. Per
quaternarium corpoream creaturam intelligimus quae
51   constat ex quattuor elementis; per ternarium intelligimus rationabilem animam. Habet enim anima rationa-
bilis esse velle scire. De septenario numero multa
54   possum dicere cur datur Palladi. *Eptas in numeris* id
est inter illos numeros qui in principio versu, id est
denario, septenarius solus et singularis est quia nec
57   gignitur.

Notes

1. *Eptas:* Greek heptas, the number seven.*Heptas in
numeris* is the text Erigena is commenting on (cf.
Dick's ed. Leipzig 1925, p.285,14).

3. **intra denarium numerum:** *intra* is regularly used
with numbers to mean 'less than', 'below', e.g. Livy
43,9: *intra dies LX.*

8. **tria<a>nullo duplicato:** Cora Lutz's text has *tria
nullo duplicata,* without any critical note, though it
makes no sense. *Nullo duplicato* as an ablative not
quite absolute ('no number being duplicated') would
help, but in view of *a nullo* in line 11 it seems better
to insert *a*, easily lost after *tria.*

25. **iuxta hunc numerum:** derived from the late uses of
iuxta to mean 'in proportion to', 'according to'; cf.
L.& S. s.v. II, B,4,5.

26. **septimani partus:** for these somewhat confusing

lines cf. Macrobius, *In Somn.* I,6,62,8; and for parallels J. Flamant, *Macrobe et le Néoplatonisme latin*, Leiden 1977, pp.342ff. There have been many attempts to trace the origins and developments of these physiological sevens - the language of all the sources is so similar that a common origin seems likely - but all one can say is that it was all commonplace by the end of the 3rd c. and was passed on to the Middle Ages not only in medical writers but also in Macrobius and Chalcidius. It looks as if Erigena has here confused *septemnestris* and *septimanus*, the seventh month delivery and the seven days for the seed to be established in the womb (according to some of the ancients). Cf esp. Censorinus, *De Die Natali*, ed. O. Jahn, 2nd ed. Amsterdam 1964, chs. 7-11.

27. caeteros: *caet-* for *cet-: ae* and *e* were pronounced the same, and are thoroughly confused, so that one finds spellings like *aecclesia* and *celum*.
  legitimi: 'proper', 'regular'.

29. aguntur: presumably 'arise', i.e. are cut. *Mutantur* refers to the change from milk to adult teeth.

32. flos et lanugo: for *flos* of the first hair of the beard, and *lanugo*, 'down', cf. the early Latin poet Pacuvius: *nunc primum opacat flore lanugo genas.* Erigena obviously got the words from our source of the Pacuvius fragment, the epitome of Festus's *De Significatione Verborum* made by Paul the Deacon for Charlemagne.

33. more: adverbially = 'usually'.
  mentis staturae: must mean 'the growings of the mind', but it is a very odd phrase.

38. epar: = *hepar, hepatis,* Greek for *iecur,* the liver; *lien* is the spleen, and *renes* the kidneys. Erigena might be airing his Greek but it is more likely that medical terminology preserved Greek names.

41. crescentis et senescentis: there may be an ellipse of *sui* after *formas*, but possibly *crescens* is used substantivally,'the crescent moon', and takes *senescentis* with it. It obviously means simply 'crescent' in the next line.

43. bicornis: from Chalcidius, *In Timaeum* 37: *de obscura crescente lumine fit bicornis, dehinc sectilis,
dehinc dimidiato maior, dehinc plena retrorsumque
maior dimidiato, sectilis, bicornis.* Cf. Isidore, *Etym.*
III,54,1. There is a strong temptation to emend *luminis sit* to *lumine fit*, in the light of Chalcidius' text,
esp. as there is no reason for the subjunctive after
siquidem.

45. planete: = *planetae*, 'the wandering stars', from the
Greek, from *planao* 'I wander'. The sun, the moon,
and the five planets visible to the naked eye, Mercury,
Venus, Mars, Jupiter and Saturn; they do not remain
'fixed' among the constellations, but 'wander'
through them, along the zodiac. The *septem spatia*
are the 'intervals', thought of spatially as well as
musically. *Tonus* is a Greek word originally meaning
'stretching of a string' and hence 'tone' or 'pitch'.

47. totam rationabilem creaturam: such ideas of
number as are here briefly referred to with respect to
three and four are set out at length in Macrobius. Four
represents body not only because of the four elements
- earth, air, fire, water - but because in Pythagorean
mathematics four points generate a solid, as three a
surface, and two a line, while one has position only.
The trinity *esse velle scire* is older than Christianity
but much used by Augustine, for example.

56. nec gignitur: *nec* = 'neither'; 'because it is not
begotten either'.

5. SAINT ANSELM

The 10th century was a time of war. The invasions of the Norsemen - the Normans - and the consequent fighting and social upheaval left little time for learning. The most interesting figure of the age, Gerbert of Aurillac, who after being archbishop successively of Rheims and Ravenna became in 999 Pope Silvester II, acquired a good knowledge not only of the Trivium but also, which was much rarer, of the Quadrivium: he learned mathematics and astronomy in northern, ex-Visigothic Spain. In the last quarter of the 11th c. there was a strong revival of interest in philosophical and theological questions. Berengarius of Tours, a pupil of Fulbert of Chartres, who had himself been a pupil of Gerbert, used the treatise on the Eucharist of Ratramn (which was attributed to Erigena) to disprove the doctrine of transubstantiation, and so re-opened the dispute and at the same time threw into stronger relief the difficult relations between reason and authority. Peter Damian reacted against the use, or misuse, of dialectical argument in theological matters, to become the complete *contemptor saeculi,* and maintained that the terms of philosophy and logic were of no use in dealing with God because of his absolute transcendence - on which point Ockham might have been sympathetic. Lanfranc, the Italian abbot of the Norman abbey of Bec who became William the Conqueror's Archbishop of Canterbury, was also hostile to the new dialecticians, but was himself well-enough trained in the schools to use dialectic against Berengarius. Of Roscelin of Compiègne, the Nominalist teacher of Abelard, something will be said in the introduction to Abelard. So we come to Anselm, who, although he was born in Aosta in Piedmont in 1033, is known as Anselm of Canterbury because he followed Lanfranc first as Abbot of Bec and then as Archbishop of Canterbury from 1093 to his death in 1109.

Anselm sought to find a middle way between the extremes of the 'Rationalists' and the anti-dialecticians. His *Monologion* was written to show his monks how the reason might properly be used to the greater glory of God. His attitude to faith and reason, and indeed his whole philosophical outlook, was essentially that of Augustine: *sicut rectus ordo exigit ut profunda fidei prius credamus quam ea praesumamus ratione discutere, ita negligentia mihi videtur, si postquam confirmati sumus in fide, non studemus quod credimus intelligere*. The earlier title of the *Monologion* was *Exemplum meditandi de ratione fidei*, and the first title of his *Proslogion* was the title of this book, *Fides Quaerens Intellectum*. He grants a good deal to the reason. The unbeliever can *ipse sibi saltem sola ratione persuadere*: convince himself at least - perhaps the implication is that it is not the way to convince others - by his reason alone. But Anselm half retracts with his caveat that he really does not mean that it is all provable apart from revelation and Scripture, only that it is plausible. The *Monologion* opens with our first extract. The argument that judgements of relative goodness, justness, 'greatness' and so on all imply a standard of comparison, a measure, of absolute good, justice, greatness, goes back to Augustine and ultimately to Plato. To argue about 'the good in itself' and even 'being itself' - *per se esse* - as Anselm does in chapter III, is to make assumptions about the 'reality' of such concepts which came more easily to the (Neo)Platonic Augustinian early Middle Ages than they would later, in the 14th c., and than they do now. Particularly the 'essential' nature of the relation between the ideas of 'greatness' and of 'the good' has Platonist overtones we might now find it difficult to recognise or acknowledge. But the arguments of Anselm still exercise the minds of philosophers, and the argument of our first extract became one of the famous 'five ways' of Aquinas' *Summa contra Gentiles*.

But it is for his ontological proof (ontology is the science of being) of God's existence that Anselm is most often remembered; that proof is set out in the second extract. It has been the subject of argument among philosophers from his day to our own. Bonaventure, Duns Scotus, Descartes, Leibniz and Hegel have been among its supporters; Aquinas, Locke and Kant among those who have rejected it. The first to attempt to refute it was Gaunilo, a monk of Marmoutiers. His argument begins by stating that *falsa dubiaque intelliguntur audita* ; and the difficulty lies in the fact that *intelligere* is ambiguous. Gaunilo distinguishes the *vox ipsa, quae res est utique vera,* from the *vocis auditae significatio* ; and he says that the thing, the object of thought, can only be said to be *in intellectu* if it is possible *illud secundum rem veram mihique notam cogitare* . When we are dealing with God, he says: *istud omnino nequeam nisi secundum vocem, secundum quam solam aut vix aut nunquam potest ullum cogitare verum* , and this because *neque..aut rem ipsam novi aut ex alia possum conicere simili, quandoquidem et tu talem asseris illam, ut esse non possit simile quicquam* . The result is that when 'that than which nothing greater can be thought of' (*illud quo maius cogitari nequit:* from now on let us refer to this as A, to avoid repetition of the phrase) is understood, it is understood *non ita ut ab illo qui novit, quid ea soleat voce significari, a quo scilicet cogitatur secundum rem vel in sola cognitione veram, verum ut ab eo qui illud non novit et solummodo cogitat secundum animi motum illius auditu vocis effectum significationemque perceptae vocis conantem effingere sibi* . The point of the argument is that the inference from *A intelligitur* to *A in intellectu est* is invalid because it is only an *intellectio* of the wrong kind which is 'in the understanding'.

As an example of the invalidity of Anselm's argumentation Gaunilo produces his now famous island, *quam..cognominant aliqui 'perditam'* , which is *terris omnibus praestantior* . The supposed argument runs: *non potes ultra dubitare insulam illam terris omnibus praestantiorem vere esse alicubi in re, quam et in intellectu tuo non ambigis esse; et quia praestantius est, non in intellectu solo sed etiam esse in re; ideo sic eam necesse est esse, quia nisi fuerit, quaecumque alia in re est terra, praestantior illa erit, ac sic ipsa iam a te praestantior intellecta praestantior non erit.* There are of course difficult questions concerning existence and essence raised by these arguments. Is it correct to say that you can add existence *in re,* or subtract it, without making any essential difference? In that case the only difference between the island which exists only *in intellectu* and that which exists *in re* is that the latter 'has' while the former 'has not' real existence; and since this is not an essential distinction the latter is in no way *praestantior* than the former. And is it a sufficient reply to say that while this may be true for contingent things, which might not exist, in which existence and essence are separate or at least separable, it is not true of God, who is necessary being, having his essence and his existence one and the same? Of all this *dicere recusabo* excusing myself in Porphyry's phrase: *altissimum enim est huiusmodi negotium, et maioris egens inquisitionis* .

As against Anselm's proof that God cannot not exist, Gaunilo replies: *cogitare autem me non esse quamdiu esse certissime scio, nescio utrum possim; sed si possim, cur non et quicquid aliud eadem certitudine scio? Si autem non possum, non est iam istud proprium Deo* . Anselm's response to this criticism is to say that if God can be thought to exist at all, then he must necessarily exist. His argument is: *A non potest cogitari esse nisi sine initio* (because if it had a beginning, something could be thought of which had no beginning, and that would be greater, and then A would not be that than which etc.); *quicquid autem potest cogitari esse et non est, potest cogitari esse per initium; non ergo A cogitari potest esse et non est; si ergo cogitari potest esse, ex necessitate est* . The premises are (1) A cannot be thought of as existing with a beginning and (2) whatever is conceivable and non-existent can be conceived as existing with a beginning(i.e. as beginning to exist); but A is conceivable, therefore etc. Anselm's second line of defence is as follows: let us grant the truth of this premise (1): *si A esset, nec actu nec intellectu posset non esse;* let us now define B as *quicquid cogitari potest et non est;* and let us grant premise (2): *si B esset, posset vel actu vel intellectu non esse.* Now *ponamus A est B; tum non esset A; ergo non est A, B;* etc. There are other arguments but they are perhaps more involved and less plausible; they can be found in the *Responsio Editoris* in the first volume of Schmitt's edition.

One of the pleasant things about this famous controversy is the spirit in which it was carried on. Gaunilo ends his *Liber pro insipiente* with the words: *cetera libelli illius tam veraciter et tam praeclare sunt magnificeque disserta, tanta denique referta utilitate et pii ac sancti affectus intimo quodam odore fragrantia, ut nullo modo propter illa quae in initiis recte quidem sensa, sed minus firmiter argumentata sunt, ista sint contemnanda; sed illa potius argumentanda robustius, ac sic omnia cum ingenti veneratione et laude suscipienda* . And Anselm says at the end of his *Responsio: gratias ago benignitati tuae et in reprehensione et in laude mei opusculi. Cum enim ea quae tibi digna susceptione videntur, tanta laude extulisti: satis apparet quia quae tibi infirma visa sunt, benevolentia non malevolentia reprehendisti* . Such charity in controversy was not perhaps typical of the age, but it was commoner then than in the somewhat acrimonious 12th c., whetted by the wits of Roscelin and Abelard, and one sees it again in Aquinas. It is the humility of the saints, which implies no toleration of irrational argument but patience and charity in dealing with men who err.

BIBLIOGRAPHY

The life by Eadmer was edited by R.W. Southern, *The Life of St. Anselm, Archbishop of Canterbury, by Eadmer* , London 1962, and the best modern life is the same scholar's *St. Anselm and his Biographer*, Cambridge 1963. A useful general work is J. Hopkins, *A Companion to the Study of St. Anselm* , Minnesota 1972, which has a good bibliography. On the ontological argument the literature is immense, but a good starting point is M.J. Charlesworth, *St. Anselm's Proslogion* , Oxford 1965; and no-one really interested should miss K. Barth, *Anselm: Fides Quaerens Intellectum* , transl. I.W. Robertson, London 1960. The works, in clear and fairly simple Latin, are beautifully available in the ed. of F.S. Schmitt, *S. Anselmi..Opera Omnia,* 6 vols, Edinburgh 1946-61, who also founded and edited until his death in 1972 the series of *Analecta Anselmiana* , volumes of essays on Anselm by many scholars.

[Cf. more recently, *Les Mutations socio-culturelles au tournant des XI-XII siècles,* ed. R. Foreville, Paris 1984, which contains several articles on Anselm]

1. Anselm: The argument to Perfection
Monologion, ch. I and II, ed. Schmitt, 1

Si quis unam naturam, summam omnium quae
sunt, solam sibi in aeterna sua beatitudine sufici-
3   entem, omnibusque rebus aliis hoc ipsum quod aliquid sunt aut quod aliquomodo bene sunt, per omnipotentem bonitatem suam dantem et facientem, aliaque
6   perplura quae de deo sive de eius creatura necessarie
credimus, aut non audiendo aut non credendo ignorat:
puto quia ea ipsa ex magna parte, si vel mediocris in-
9   genii est, potest ipse sibi saltem sola ratione persuadere. Quod cum multis modis facere possit, unam
ponam, quem illi aestimo esse promptissimum.
12   Etenim cum omnes frui solis iis appetant quae bona
putant: in promptu est, ut aliquando mentis oculum
convertat ad investigandum illud, unde sunt bona ea
15   ipsa, quae non appetit nisi quia iudicat esse bona, ut
deinde ratione ducente et illo prosequente ad ea quae
irrationabiliter ignorat, rationabiliter proficiat. In quo
18   tamen si quid dixero quod maior non monstret auctoritas: sic volo accipi ut, quamvis ex rationibus quae
mihi videbuntur, quasi necessarium concludatur, non
21   ob hoc tamen omnino necessarium, sed tantum sic
interim videri posse dicatur.
    Facile est igitur ut aliquis sic secum tacitus dicat:
24   cum tam innumerabilia bona sint, quorum tam multam
diversitatem et sensibus corporeis experimur et ratione
mentis discernimus: estne credendum esse unum ali-
27   quid, per quod unum sint bona quaecumque bona
sunt, an sunt bona alia per aliud? Certissimum quidem
et omnibus est volentibus advertere perspicuum quia,
30   quaecumque dicuntur aliquid ita, ut ad invicem magis
vel minus aut aequaliter dicantur: per aliquid dicuntur,
quod non aliud et aliud sed idem intelligitur in diver-
33   sis, sive in illis aequaliter sive inaequaliter considere-
tur. Nam quaecumque iusta dicuntur ad invicem sive
pariter sive magis vel minus, non possunt intelligi
36   iusta nisi per iustitiam, quae non est aliud et aliud in
diversis. Ergo cum certum sit quod omnia bona, si ad

invicem conferantur, aut aequaliter aut inaequaliter
39   sint bona, necesse est, ut omnia sint per aliquid bona,
quod intelligitur idem in diversis bonis, licet aliquando videantur bona dici alia per aliud.
42   Per aliud enim videtur dici bonus equus quia fortis
est, et per aliud bonus equus quia velox est. Cum
enim dici videatur bonus per fortitudinem et bonus per
45   velocitatem, non tamen idem videtur esse fortitudo et
velocitas. Verum si equus, quia est fortis aut velox,
idcirco bonus est: quomodo fortis et velox latro malus
48   est? Potius igitur, quemadmodum fortis et velox latro
ideo malus est quia noxius est, ita fortis et velox
equus idcirco bonus est quia utilis est. Et quidem nihil
51   solet putari bonum nisi aut propter aliquam utilitatem,
ut bona dicitur salus et quae saluti prosunt, aut propter
quamlibet honestatem, sicut pulchritudo aestimatur
54   bona et quae pulchritudinem iuvant. Sed quoniam iam
perspecta ratio nullo potest dissolvi pacto, necesse est
omne quoque utile vel honestum, si vere bona sunt,
57   per idipsum esse bona, per quod necesse est esse
cuncta bona, quidquid illud sit.
Quis autem dubitet illud ipsum, per quod cuncta
60   sunt bona, esse magnum bonum? Illud igitur est
bonum per seipsum, quoniam omne bonum est per
ipsum. Ergo consequitur, ut omnia alia bona sint per
63   aliud quam quod ipsa sunt, et ipsum solum per se-
ipsum.At nullum bonum, quod per aliud est, aequale
aut maius est eo bono, quod per se est bonum. Illud
66   itaque solum est summe bonum quod solum est per se
bonum. Id enim summum est, quod sic supereminet
aliis, ut nec par habeat nec praestantius. Sed quod est
69   summe bonum, est etiam summe magnum. Est igitur
unum aliquid summe bonum et summe magnum, id
est summum omnium quae sunt.
72   Quemadmodum autem inventum est aliquid esse
summe bonum, quoniam cuncta bona per unum aliquid sunt bona, quod est bonum per seipsum: sic ex
75   necessitate colligitur aliquid esse summe magnum,
quoniam quaecumque magna sunt, per unum aliquid
magna sunt, quod magnum est per seipsum. Dico

78 autem non magnum spatio, ut est corpus aliquod; sed
quod quanto maius tanto melius est aut dignius, ut est
sapientia. Et quoniam non potest esse summe mag-
81 num nisi id quod est summe bonum, necesse est aliquid esse maximum et optimum, id est summum
omnium quae sunt.

Notes

4. **aut:** probably the sort of *aut* usually used with *vero*
in CL meaning 'or indeed'; as L.& S. has it, 'to con-
nect a more important thought'. It is clearly not disjunctive.

6. **perplura:** the CL form for 'very many' is *permulti;
perplures* is a 4th-c. invention.
creatura: a wholly Christian derivative from *creare*.
It has three meanings: the act of creating, the whole
that is created, and the separate thing created; in
English creation, Creation , a creature. These
'meanings' are not always separable, and the first two
seem to be implied here.

7. **audiendo..credendo:** 'participial' gerunds; see
note on line 45 of the first extract from Augustine.

13. **in promptu est, ut:** a construction not perhaps
exemplified in CL, but there are plenty of parallels
such as *alicui propositum est, ut* without any
suggestion of command. The natural extension of
such a use of *ut* is to such expressions as *facile est
igitur ut..dicat* (line 23) and *ergo consequitur ut..sint*
(line 62).

16. **illo prosequente:** 'and proceeding (or accompany-
ing him) to that point'.

17. **in quo tamen:** this sentence was added by Anselm
after his first version was published. It clearly wea-
kens the apparent assertion of the independence of the
reason.

30. **quaecumque dicuntur aliquid ita, ut:** 'whatever
things are said to be something (e.g. red) in such a
way that they are called that more or less or equally
with respect to one another'. It is easy to see why

another hand inserted *ad* before *aliquid:* 'whatever are predicated of something in such a way..', but it is not necessary to the sense and *quaecumque iusta dicuntur* in line 34 shows that the text is correct. *Dicere* = 'call', 'name' is common in CL poetry.

48. Potius igitur: 'It would be better then to say..' not that a horse is good because of its strength or speed but because of its usefulness.

2. Anselm: The Ontological Argument
Proslogion I-III, ed. Schmitt, 1

Fateor, domine, et gratias ago, quia creasti in me hanc
imaginem tuam, ut tui memor te cogitem, te amem.
3 Sed sic est abolita attritione vitiorum, sic est offuscata
fumo peccatorum, ut non possit facere ad quod facta
est, nisi tu renoves et reformes eam. Non tento, do-
6 mine, penetrare altitudinem tuam, quia nullatenus
comparo illi intellectum meum; sed desidero aliquatenus intelligere veritatem tuam, quam credit et amat
9 cor meum. Neque enim quaero intelligere ut credam,
sed credo ut intelligam. Nam et hoc credo: quia 'nisi
credidero, non intelligam'.
12 Ergo, domine, qui das fidei intellectum, da mihi, ut
quantum scis expedire intelligam, quia es sicut credimus, et hoc es quod credimus. Et quidem credimus te
15 esse aliquid quo nihil maius cogitari possit. An ergo
non est aliqua talis natura, quia 'dixit insipiens in
corde suo: non est Deus'? Sed certe ipse idem insipi-
18 ens, cum audit hoc ipsum quod dico: 'aliquid quo
maius nihil cogitari potest', intelligit quod audit; et
quod intelligit in intellectu eius est, etiam si non intel-
21 ligat illud esse. Aliud enim est rem esse in intellectu,
aliud intelligere rem esse. Nam cum pictor praecogitat
quae facturus est, habet quidem in intellectu, sed non-
24 dum intelligit esse quod nondum fecit. Cum vero iam
pinxit, et habet in intellectu et intelligit esse quod iam
fecit. Convincitur ergo etiam insipiens esse vel in
27 intellectu aliquid quo nihil maius cogitari potest, quia
hoc cum audit intelligit, et quidquid intelligitur in
intellectu est. Et certe id quo maius cogitari nequit non
30 potest esse in solo intellectu. Si enim vel in solo intellectu est, potest cogitari esse et in re, quod maius est.
Si ergo id quo maius cogitari non potest est in solo in-
33 tellectu: id ipsum quo maius cogitari non potest, est
quo maius cogitari potest. Sed certe hoc esse non
potest. Existit ergo procul dubio aliquid quo maius
36 cogitari non valet, et in intellectu et in re.
Quod utique sic vere est, ut nec cogitari possit non

esse. Nam potest cogitari esse aliquid, quod non
39 possit cogitari non esse; quod maius est quam quod
non esse cogitari potest. Quare si id quo maius nequit
cogitari, potest cogitari non esse: id ipsum quo maius
42 cogitari nequit, non est id quo maius cogitari nequit;
quod convenire non potest. Sic ergo vere est aliquid
quo maius cogitari non potest, ut nec cogitari possit
45 non esse.

Et hoc es tu, domine deus noster. Sic ergo vere es,
domine deus meus, ut nec cogitari possis non esse. Et
48 merito. Si enim aliqua mens posset cogitare aliquid
melius te, ascenderet creatura super creatorem, et iudi-
caret de creatore; quod valde est absurdum. Et quidem
51 quidquid est aliud praeter te solum, potest cogitari non
esse. Solus igitur verissime omnium, et ideo maxime
omnium habes esse: quia quidquid aliud est non sic
54 vere, et idcirco minus habet esse. Cur itaque 'dixit insipiens in corde suo: non est deus', cum tam in promptu sit rationali menti te maxime omnium esse? Cur,
57 nisi quia stultus et insipiens?

Notes

2. **tui memor..te amem:** cf. Augustine, *De Trin.*
XIV, 12,15: *haec igitur trinitas mentis non propterea
dei est imago qui sui meminit mens ac intelligit ac
diligit se; sed quia potest etiam meminisse et
intelligere et amare a quo facta est.*
4. **ut non possit..:** man lost by the Fall not his free
will nor his capacity to know the good that should be
his aim, but his power to act meritoriously and to
attain that good. Cf. Aug., *De Div.Quaest. ad
Simplic.,* I,2,2:*et multis locis hoc saepe testatur
(sc.Apostolus) fidei gratiam praeponens operibus..ut
scilicet non se quisque arbitretur ideo percepisse
gratiam qui bene operatus est, sed bene operari non
posse, nisi per fidem percepit gratiam.* Cf. also
Erigena, *De Praed.*V, 4: *ipsa libertas post peccatum in
tantum vitiata est ut poena eius impediatur ne aut recte
vivere velit aut si velit non possit.* Cf. Rom.7,14-25.

ad quod: = *id ad quod;* the omission of the antecedent demonstrative is not common in CL except
where no prepositions are involved (cf. line 23: *quae
facturus est).* But cf. Ovid, *Rem.Am.,* 43: *discite
sanari per quem didicistis amare;* and Cic., *Att.* V,11,
6: *nunc redeo ad quae mihi mandas.* In these instances
the case of the antecedent and the relative pronoun are
the same, but cf. *a quo* in the quotation from Augustine in the note to line 2.

12. **fidei:** did Anselm intend a genitive or a dative here
or both? 'Cases' are partly at least grammarians'
fictions.

16. **aliqua:** a very weak 'any'; *talis* alone would have
been enough.
    dixit insipiens..: Ps. 14,1.

26. **vel:** emphatic, with no disjunctive force; so too in
line 30. It may have some of the force of *saltem* = at
least; cf. Cic., *Fam.* XI,22,2: *qua re etsi minus veram
causam habebis, tamen vel probabilem aliquam poteris inducere* . In LL *vel* often means no more than
'and' with no sense of disjunction.

37. **sic vere est:** the *sic* should probably be taken with
the clause *vere est* and the following *ut* as a consecutive construction, rather than directly with *vere* as
if = *tam;* so too in line 43. But uses such as this
obviously lead to the use of *sic* with adjectives and
adverbs as equivalent to *tam,* as it is (*si*) in the Romance languages. *Vere* marks out *est* as existential.

43. **convenire:** = *congruere,* 'to be consistent','to agree'
as in Ovid, *Met.* II,846: *non bene conveniunt, nec in
una sede morantur / maiestas et amor.*

47. **deus meus:** *meus* as the vocative instead of *mi* is
very occasionally used by poets in CL, e.g. Plautus,
Cist. 53, and Virgil, *Aen.* 6,835, but it only becomes
common in ecclesiastical Latin, especially in conjunction with *domine* (or occasionally *dominus*) and
deus.

50. **de creatore:** *de* after *iudicare* is rare in CL but is
typical of the medieval preference for prepositional
constructions (probably arising from popular speech

where it was partly due to weak pronunciation and consequent confusion of case endings). Cf. Cic., *Mil.* 2,4: *de bene meritis civibus potestas iudicandi.*

6. ABELARD

When St. Anselm died in 1109 Peter Abelard was already thirty, and teaching in Paris, where there were now gathered students from all over Europe to hear the great masters in theology and logic. One hundred years later this gathering of masters and students was officially recognised as the University of Paris (*Universitas magistrorum scolariumque*) - where the word *universitas* merely means 'the whole body', as a legal entity which can be held responsible for its members - the first university in Europe. The power of Abelard's teaching had much to do with the speed with which Paris flourished into becoming the cultural centre of north-west Europe.

He was born at Le Pallet near Nantes but though he was the eldest son he renounced chivalry for philosophy and studied under the best masters of the day: Roscelin of Compiègne, William of Champeaux, Anselm of Laon. He stayed with each only long enough to disagree, and trusting in his own superlative skill in dialectic set up his own school in, or rather near what was then the city of Paris, on the Mont Ste. Geneviève. There he gathered a great number of students, attracted by the forcefulness and originality of his teaching, a forcefulness and originality which brought upon him the condemnations of two councils, that of Soissons in 1121 and Sens in 1140. Before the first council falls the story of his love for and marriage with Héloise - *occasio quaedam satis nota*, as Otto of Freising called it - and two years after the second Abelard was dead.

His importance in the history of medieval philosophy has always been recognised, at least since Cousin and Rémusat in the early 19th century, because of the part he played in the argument over the nature of universals - an argument as old as Plato revived in the early Middle Ages and looming so large in the 12th century that some earlier historians saw medieval philosophy only in terms of it. But Abelard's impor-tance lies in his standing at the head of two streams of later development, which culminate the one in the works of Aquinas and Duns Scotus, the other in the logic of Ockham and Burleigh. For though Abelard was not the first to apply the dialectic of the schools to theological enquiry, though he certainly did not make such application respectable - the mighty saintliness of Bernard of

Clairvaux saw to that - yet his was the spirit and the approach and the method which despite conservative opposition was to produce among its fruits the 13th-century Summas. His *Sic et Non* (Yes and No), a collection and discussion of contradictory *auctoritates* , heads a tradition of teaching known later as 'the Scholastic method', the way of the Schools. His work in logic began a line of formal logical teaching in the Arts faculties (through which a student passed on his way to theology, law or medicine) which, through such dialecticians as William Shyreswood, Lambert of Auxerre and Peter of Spain (the author of the most popular textbook of logic for many centuries) led to the great 14th-century works wherein modern logicians are finding some of their recent discoveries anticipated.

Our first extract is concerned with the problem of universals and Abelard's views on it. The problem is stated in Porphyry's *Isagogê* (a Greek word meaning 'introduction', the book being introductory to Aristotle's *Categories*) and in Boethius' translation ran thus: *mox de generibus ac speciebus illud quidem, sive subsistunt sive in solis nudisque intellectibus posita sunt sive subsistentia corporalia sunt an incorporalia et utrum separata a sensibilibus an in sensibilibus posita et circa ea constantia, dicere recusabo. Altissimum enim est huiusmodi negotium et maioris egens inquisitionis.* Boethius in his commentary gave Plato's and Aristotle's answers but did not decide between the two, giving as his own opinion the somewhat ambiguous statement: *itaque haec (sc.* genus et species) *sunt quidem in singularibus, cogitantur vero universalia nihilque aliud species esse putanda est nisi cogitatio collecta ex individuorum dissimilium numero substantiali similitudine, genus vero cogitatio collecta ex specierum similitudine.* What is a 'substantial likeness of individuals differing in number'? It is what makes it possible to call this a chair, and this a chair, and this.. and so on. Which seems sensible until one asks 'What is "it"?' - when "it" has so far no sort of status. The question is, what sort of status has 'man' in 'Every man is mortal'? What is the word 'man' doing in that sort of sentence? Does it actually 'stand for' anything? In the 11th century a school of Nominalists arose, begun, it was said, by an unknown John the Sophist, but founded, so far as history is concerned, by Roscelin of Compiègne. Roscelin, an acute and bitter mind, was born about 1050, taught at Loches - where Abelard was one of his students - and later at Besancon and Tours, and died about 1125. His Nominalism caused some trouble with the theologians, and he was accused of tritheism, of saying that there were three gods. But he does not appear to have been condemned by any council, and certainly died a respected member of the Church. The chief representative of the opposing school of Realists was William of Champeaux, who had also been Abelard's master. Some twenty years younger than Roscelin, he studied first in Paris, where Abelard heard him and forced him to modify his extreme realism, and after five years at the Abbey of St. Victor he died as Bishop of Châlons-sur-Marne in 1121. Briefly the Realist answer to the problem of universals was that the universal, e.g. 'man', was a real thing (hence Realism) which actually existed in its own right (for Plato, at least at first, only this, the Form or Idea, did exist, and all else was only seeming, becoming). Individual men were what they were, men, because of some kind of imitation of or participation in the universal. The Nominalist attitude of Roscelin was that the universal was only a word, a mere sound, having no other existence - a mere *flatus vocis* Anselm said they called it. Individual men exist, but there is no such thing as 'man'. Abelard's answer is called 'Conceptualist' by the pigeon-holers - the medieval thinkers were, following the Philosopher, Aristotle, great classifiers, so we do them no injustice - *nam et res diversas per nominationem quodammodo significant* (sc. universals) *non constituendo tamen intellectum de eis surgentem, sed ad singulas pertinentem. Ut haec vox 'homo' et singulos nominat ex communi causa, quod scilicet homines sunt* - he here refers to the common cause of the application of a universal (the *impositio* in the dialectician's language) to many things taken singly, what he calls their *status* , the *status hominis* being simply *esse hominem* , 'being a man', which is not a separate thing - *propter quam universale dicitur, et intellectum quemdam constituit communem, non proprium, ad singulos scilicet pertinentem, quorum communem concipit similitudinem.* This makes the universal a concept formed in the mind by abstraction from the common likenesses of individuals; it exists only in the mind and not in the object. This is not the whole answer and it leaves many difficulties, while one Platonic notion is, moreover, more or less untouched by the controversy: the Ideas which the Demiurge of the *Timaeus* had taken as patterns for the fashioning of the world were now, via the Neoplatonists and Augustine, located in the Logos, the Second Person of the Trinity, 'through whom all things were made', as the archetypes of the Creation. Thus the *universale ante rem*, in one sense, still existed for all these controversialists; it was over the nature of the *universale in re* or *post rem* that disagreement occurred, in which the distinction between *res* and *voces* which coloured much logical argument in the 11th and early 12th centuries played an essential part. The effect of Abelard's treatment of the problem was to shift it from the metaphysical to the logical plane, or at any rate to separate the logical from the metaphysical issues involved.

The second extract is from Abelard's *Scito te ipsum*, his *Ethics* (the Latin is the translation of the Delphic 'Know thyself'). For the work, its context and importance, see D.E. Luscombe's introduction to his edition. The extract raises in an acute form the problem of intention. When Jesus said (Mt. 5,27-28) 'Ye have heard that it was said by them of old time,"Thou shalt not commit adultery"; but I say unto you, That whosoever looketh on a woman to lust after her hath committed adultery with her already in his heart', did he mean that it was really as sinful to 'lust after' as actually to commit adultery? Or is it as Augustine and Anselm say, that *non eos* (sc. the desires of the flesh) *sentire sed eis consentire peccatum est* ? Or is there a middle position, as Augustine says elsewhere, *inest peccatum cum delectaris; regnat, si consenseris* ? (See Luscombe, p.14, note 1). The questions of intention and guilt have exercised moral philosophers and theologians until the present day. The 12th century was much concerned with ethical problems, and Abelard's work is the most important and stimulating of that lively age, produced as it was by one of the most stimulating minds of the Middle Ages.

BIBLIOGRAPHY
On Roscelin: F. Picavet, *Roscelin, philosophe et théologien* , Paris 1911; on the 12th c. see especially G. Paré, A. Brunet, P. Tremblay, *La Renaissance du douzième siècle. Les écoles et l'enseignement* , Paris 1933. On Abelard see D.E. Luscombe, *The School of Peter Abelard* , Cambridge 1969, and the edition of the *Ethics* used here; also R.E. Weingart, *The Logic of Divine Love* , Oxford 1970. His *Sic et Non* has been edited by B. Boyer and R. McKeon, Chicago 1976. For the universities and much else see H. Rashdall's*Medieval Universities*, revised by F.M. Powicke and A.B. Emden, Oxford 1936.

1. Abelard: Universals
Logica 'Ingredientibus', ed. B. Geyer, Peter Abaelards
Philosophische Schriften, Münster 1919, p.22

De forma autem ipsa, in quam scilicet intellectus dirigitur, non absurde dubitatur, utrum eam quoque nomen
3   significet, quod tam auctoritate quam ratione confir-
mari videtur.

In primos namque *Constructionum* Priscianus, cum
6   communem impositionem universalium ad individua
praemonstrasset, quandam aliam ipsorum significatio-
nem, de forma scilicet communi, visus est subiunx-
9   isse dicens: 'ad generales et speciales rerum formas,
quae in mente divina intelligibiliter constituuntur,
antequam in corpora prodirent, haec quoque propria
12   possunt esse, quibus genera vel species naturae rerum
demonstrantur'. Hoc enim loco de Deo sic agitur quasi de artifice aliquid composituro, qui rei componen-
15   dae exemplarem formam, ad similitudinem cuius operetur, anima praeconcipit, quae tunc in corpus pro-
cedere dicitur, cum ad similitudinem eius res vera
18   componitur. Haec autem communis conceptio bene
Deo adscribitur, non homini; quia opera illa generales
vel speciales naturae status sunt, non artificis, ut
21   homo, anima vel lapis Dei, domus autem vel gladius
hominis. Unde haec naturae non sunt opera domus et
gladius, sicut illa, nec eorum vocabula substantiae
24   sunt, sed accidentis atque ideo nec genera sunt nec
specialissima. Inde etiam bene divinae menti, non
humanae huius modi per abstractionem conceptiones
27   adscribuntur, quia homines, qui per sensus tantum res
cognoscunt, vix aut nunquam ad huius modi simpl-
icem intelligentiam conscendunt et ne pure rerum
30   naturas concipiant, accidentium exterior sensualitas
impedit. Deus vero cui omnia per se patent, quae condidit, quique ea antequam sint, novit, singulos status
33   in se ipsis distinguit nec ei sensus impedimento est,
qui solus veram habet intelligentiam. Unde homines
in his quae sensu non attractaverunt, magis opinionem
36   quam intelligentiam habere contingit, quod ipso expe-

rimento discimus. Cogitantes enim de aliqua civitate
non visa, cum advenerimus, eam nos aliter quam sit
39   excogitasse invenimus.

Ita etiam credo de intrinsecis formis quae ad sensus
non veniunt, qualis est rationalitas et mortalitas, pater-
42   nitas, sessio, magis nos opinionem habere. Quaelibet
tamen quorumlibet existentium nomina, quantum in
ipsis est, intellectum magis quam opinionem generant,
45   quia secundum aliquas rerum naturas vel proprietates
inventor ea imponere intendit, etsi nec ipse bene exco-
gitare sciret rei naturam aut proprietatem. Communes
48   autem has conceptiones inde generales vel speciales
Priscianus vocat, quod eas nobis generalia vel speci-
alia nomina utcumque insinuant. Ad quas quidem
51   conceptiones quasi propria nomina esse dicit ipsa universalia, quae licet confusae significationis sint, quantum ad nominatas essentias, ad communem illam con-
54   ceptionem statim dirigunt animum auditoris sicut propria nomina ad rem unam quam significant. Ipse quoque Porphyrius, cum ait quaedam constitui ex materia
57   et forma, quaedam ad similitudinem materiae et
formae, hanc conceptionem intellexisse videtur, cum
ait ad similitudinem materiae et formae, de quo
60   plenius suo loco dicetur. Boethius quoque cum ait
cogitationem collectam ex similitudine multorum
genus esse vel speciem, eandem communem concep-
63   tionem intellexisse videtur. In qua etiam sententia
Platonem fuisse quidam autumant, ut videlicet illas
ideas communes, quas in noy ponit, genera vel
66   species appellaret. In quo fortasse Boethius eum ab
Aristotele dissensisse commemorat, ubi is ait eum
voluisse genera et species ceteraque non solum intel-
69   ligi universalia, verum etiam esse ac praeter corpora
subsistere, ac si diceret illas communes conceptiones,
quas separatas a corporibus in noy constituit, eum in-
72   tellexisse universalia, non fortasse accipientem universale secundum communem praedicationem, sicut
facit Aristoteles, sed magis secundum communem
75   multorum similitudinem. Illa namque conceptio de
pluribus nullo modo praedicari videtur, sicut nomen

quod pluribus singillatim aptatur.

Notes

5.   in primos..Priscianus: Priscian the grammarian
was born in Caesarea in Mauretania early in the 6th c.
Though he wrote many shorter rhetorical and grammatical works, his importance for the Middle Ages lay
in the 18 books of his *Institutiones Grammaticae* , the
fullest and most advanced grammar textbook of the
schools, which contained many remnants of the
ancient Stoics'logic and linguistic theory of great
importance in the development of 12th-c. ideas. This
grammar included two books on syntax, XVII and
XVIII, sometimes separately copied and entitled
together *De Constructione, sive de Ordinatione
Partium Orationis* . So Book XVII was the 'first book
of Priscian's *Constructions* '. The reference is to ch.
24 of that book. Priscian's grammar is in vols II and
III of H. Keil's *Grammatici Latini* , Leipzig 1857-70.

6.   impositionem: cf. Varro, *Ling. Lat.* VIII,5; X,51,
61; *impositio* is used of the simple application of a
word, a name, to a thing in the nominative case: *duo
igitur omnino verborum principia, impositio et
declinatio..*

12.   naturae rerum: 'the world', as in Lucretius' title.

14.   composituro: a late use of a future participle instead
of a relative clause with its origins perhaps in less
'literary' Latin than Cicero's: Sallust has examples.

16.   anima praeconcipit: *animus* is more often used of
the mind, *anima* of the soul, but no firm distinction
can be drawn at any period. *Praeconcipio* is formed
on the analogy of such words as *praecognosco, prae-
cogito* , but it seems to be a 12th-c. invention.

18.   haec..conceptio: i.e. the *forma communi* of line
8. *Conceptio* in the sense of 'conception', 'idea' is
not CL, but transitional uses are such as Varro, *Ling.
Lat.* fr.1: *res autem ipsa quae iam verbum non est
neque verbi in mente conceptio;* and Aulus Gellius
XI, 13,9: *quae (verba) nasci oririque ex ipsa rei*

conceptione debebant.

19. opera illa: i.e. God's works, those he made (*quasi de artifice*) from the patterns in his mind, from the *communis forma* or *conceptio* , in the sense of the *universale ante rem.*

20. status: 'existents' or 'essences': see note on line 4 of the second Boethius extract.

25. specialissima: originally and more often *species specialissima:* the *infima species*, those species which are not also genera to lower divisions (man, donkey etc.). Cf. Boethius' translation of Porphyry: *est autem generalissima quidem, super quod nullum ultra aliud superveniens genus, specialissima autem, post quod non est alia inferior species.*

26. abstractionem: in CL only spatially, 'drawing away' (from *abstrahere*) or meaning an abduction. Boethius first used it in the present sense in translating Aristotle's logic, but cf. also Isidore, *Etym.* II, 24,14: *abstracta enim qualitas dicitur, quam intellectu a materia separantes..in sola ratiocinatione tractamus.*

30. sensualitas: normally used (by Tertullian first) in an active sense, meaning the capacity for feeling = Greek *aisthetikos;* here it is passive = *aisthetos*, the capacity for being felt, or experienced through the senses.

35. attractaverunt: usually *attrect-* in CL; 'touch' or 'seek to touch', from the Vulgate.

36. contingit (homines..habere): in CL *contingere* is used with the dative, and sometimes in poetry and later writings with an infinitive as well, e.g. Hor.,*Ep.* 1,17,36:*non cuivis homini contingit adire Corinthum.* It seems first to be used with accusative and infinitive in Aulus Gellius IX,3,5: *quod eum nasci contigit temporibus vitae tuae;* cf. Amm. Marc. XVIII,2,14 and the Vulgate, Acts 28,8: *contigit autem patrem Publii febribus et dysenteria iacere.*

38. eam nos aliter..: the order of words is perhaps confusing; the construction is *invenimus nos eam excogitasse aliter quam sit.*

40. de intrinsecis formis: 'man', 'chair', 'house' and

so on are *extrinsecae formae* , abstracted from objects
of sense-perception; 'mortality', 'paternity' and so
forth are abstracted from qualities and relationships,
themselves concepts or ideas in the mind. *Intrinsecus*
is an adverb only in CL and is first used as an adjective in Cassiodorus, *In Ps*.118,82: *constat ergo
oculos istos esse intellectuales, id est lumina cordis
intrinseca.*

50. **insinuant:** probably simply = 'make known', with a
possible idea of 'inserting' or 'stealing into'.
ad quas: *ad* is used by grammarians in this technical
sense - *nomina ad aliquid dicta*, names used for (in
relation to) something.

55. **ipse quoque Porphyrius:** Geyer, p.79ff., where
Abelard, following Boethius (*In Porph.ed*.II, p.267,
3) draws a parallel between the statue of a man, made
of matter, bronze; and form, the human form impress-
ed in the bronze by the sculptor, in regard to which
'matter' and 'form' are properly used; and man, who
as a rational animal is composed of matter, the genus
animal , and form, the *differentia*, rationality, where
'matter' and 'form' are used by analogy, since the
matter in this case is not really and temporally prior to
the compound of matter and form, but only 'naturally'
prior: *unde homo proprie ex materia et forma non
constat sicut statua, sed similitudinem tenet constituti
ex materia et forma. Sicut enim ibi aes quod tempore
quoque praecessit, per figuram quam suscepit, factum
est statua, sic animalis substantia naturaliter prior
homine, per differentiam quam habet homo ipse, est.*
So Boethius: *quemadmodum statua ex materia est
aeris, forma autem figura, sic et homo communis et
specialis ex materia quidem similiter consistit genere,
ex forma autem differentia, totum autem hoc animal
rationale mortale homo est, quemadmodum illic
statua.*

60. **Boethius quoque:** *In Porph. ed.* II, p.166,14.

64. **ut videlicet..appellaret:** in CL *ut* seems only to
be used = 'because' after *non* or *sed*, e.g. Cic., *Att.
XIV,17,4: earum exempla tibi misi non ut deliberarem*

..sed quod..; here the subjunctive may be regarded as sub-oblique after *autumant.*

65. noy: this should be *nou* , genitive; but this form and *nous* , nominative, seem to be the only forms used by Abelard, who was confessedly ignorant of Greek. The problem was the transliteration of the Greek upsilon, which was sometimes y as in *psyche* , and sometimes u as in *nous.*

67. ubi is ait: *In Porph. ed.* II, p.167,12.

68. intelligi universalia: 'to be understood to be universals'; a CL use of *intellegere* , though rare: cf. Cic.,*Tusc.* III,18,41: *non habeo quod intellegam bonum illud.*

70. subsistere: 'subsist', 'continue to exist', 'remain'; cf. Pliny *N.H.*, XXXIII,i,7,30: *equitum nomen subsistebat in turmis equorum publicorum;* so it simply came to be used as 'to be' from the 4th c.

73. communem praedicationem..similitudinem: the opposition is between *communis praedicatio* , the abstraction and naming of the form and the predication of the name of many things, where the 'universal' only exists as a mental concept, and *communis similitudo* , which is in the things themselves.

75. illa namque: that is, although the name itself, 'man' for example, is fitted to be applied to many things taken singly, it is not itself the universal (as against Roscelin's Nominalism); the universal itself, the *communis conceptio,* whether the abstracted form or the eternal idea, is not predicated of anything.

2. Abelard: Act and Intention
Scito te ipsum, ed D.E. Luscombe, Peter Abelard's Ethics,
Oxford 1971.

Quod de luxuria diximus, hoc et de gula videamus.
Transit aliquis iuxta ortum alterius, et conspectis
3   delectabilibus fructibus in concupiscentiam eorum
incidit, nec tamen concupiscentiae suae consentit, ut
inde aliquid furto vel rapina auferat, quamquam de-
6   lectacione cibi in magnum desiderium mens eius sit
accensa. Ubi autem desiderium ibi procul dubio
voluntas consistit. Desiderat itaque fructus illius esum
9   in quo delectationem esse non dubitat. Ipsa quippe
suae infirmitatis natura compellitur id desiderare quod
inscio domino vel non permittente non licet accipere.
12   Desiderium ille reprimit, non extinguit, sed quia non
trahitur ad consensum, non incurrit peccatum.
Quorsum autem ista? Ut denique pateat in talibus
15   ipsam quoque voluntatem vel desiderium faciendi
quod non licet nequaquam dici peccatum, sed ipsum
potius, ut diximus, consensum. Tunc vero consen-
18   timus ei quod non licet, cum nos ab eius perpetratione
nequaquam retrahimus parati penitus, si daretur facul-
tas, illud perficere. In hoc itaque proposito quisquis
21   reperitur reatus perfectionem incurrit nec operis effectus super additus ad peccati augmentum quicquam
addit, sed iam apud Deum eque reus est qui ad hoc
24   peragendum quantum valet nititur, et quantum in se
est illud peragit, ac si, ut beatus Augustinus meminit,
in opere quoque ipso esset deprehensus.
27   Cum autem voluntas peccatum non sit et non numquam inviti, ut diximus, peccata committamus, nonnulli tamen omne peccatum voluntarium esse dicunt,
30   in quo et quandam differentiam peccati a voluntate in-
veniunt, cum aliud voluntas aliud voluntarium dicatur,
hoc est, aliud voluntas aliud quod per voluntatem
33   committitur. At vero si peccatum dicimus quod proprie dici peccatum prefati sumus, hoc est, contemp-
tum Dei sive consensum in eo quod credimus propter

36 Deum dimittendum, quomodo dicimus peccatum esse
voluntarium, hoc est, nos velle Deum contempnere,
quod est peccare, vel deteriores fieri aut dignos
39 dampnatione effici?
Quamvis enim velimus facere id quod debere puniri
scimus vel unde puniri digni simus, non tamen puniri
42 volumus, in hoc ipso manifeste iniqui quod hoc volumus facere quod est iniquum, nec tamen penae quae
iusta est subire volumus equitatem. Displicet pena
45 quae iusta est, placet actio quae est iniusta. Sepe etiam
contingit ut cum velimus concumbere cum ea quam
scimus coniugatam, specie illius illecti, nequaquam
48 tamen adulterari cum ea vellemus quam esse coniugatam nollemus. Multi e contrario sunt qui uxores
potentum ad gloriam suam eo magis appetunt quia
51 talium uxores sunt quam si essent innuptae, et magis
adulterari quam fornicari cupiunt, hoc est, magis
quam minus excedere. Sunt quos omnino piget in
54 consensum concupiscentiae vel malam voluntatem
trahi, et hoc ex infirmitate carnis velle coguntur quod
nequaquam vellent velle. Quomodo ergo hic consen-
57 sus quem habere non volumus voluntarius dicetur, ut
secundum quosdam, velut dictum est, omne peccatum
dicamus voluntarium, profecto non video nisi volun-
60 tarium intelligamus ad exclusionem necessarii, cum
videlicet nullum peccatum inevitabile sit, vel voluntarium dicamus quod ex aliqua procedat voluntate. Nam
63 et si ille qui coactus dominum suum occidit, non
habuit voluntatem in occisione, id tamen ex aliqua
commisit voluntate cum videlicet mortem evadere vel
66 differre vellet.

Notes
2. **iuxta ortum:** *ortum* = *hortum:* the occurrence or
non-occurrence of h in medieval texts is a random
business, dependent on the whims as much of editors
as of scribes. *Iuxta* = 'alongside', 'along the side of'.
There must be here a reminiscence of Augustine's
theft of the pears in *Confessions* IV.

4. **consentit:** and *consensum* in line 17 etc. In the modern sense of 'consent' only in the Vulgate and later, but it is a natural enough extension of CL meanings. The *eorum* in the same line is of course the same fruit as the *conspectis..fructibus* earlier, but it is a fairly typical medieval ablative 'absolute'.

6. **eius:** presumably refers either to *cibi* or *aliquid* , but it could just = *sua*.

10. **compellitur id desiderare:** the infinitive after *compellere* is rare and poetic in CL but used later in legal contexts.

12. **ille:** has already become merely 'he' - *il* in Romance languages.

18. **perpetratione:** Tertullian and later; the verb *perpetro* seems to have dropped out of use (vulgar?) in the golden age.

19. **nequaquam:** here and elsewhere probably virtually = *non* , by the sort of weakening which reduced *minime* to *non* much earlier.

21. **reatus:** genitive. In the sense of 'guilt' only in the Vulgate and Christian writers. *Incurrit* with the accusative without *in* is also late and Christian.

23. **eque:** = *aeque* . Luscombe's translation cannot be right: *ac si* must be taken with *eque* , and the last part of the sentence runs: 'but already before God he is guilty who strives to do this so far as he is able, and so far as is in his power does do it, just as if (as the blessed Augustine says) he had been caught in the very act as well'. The point is that the consent to the temptation, and the intention to commit the act produce the guilt, and actually doing the act adds nothing to the sin, the guilt before God. The passage in Augustine is *De libero arbitrio, i,3*.

27. **voluntas:** the Latin is wider in its connotation than the English 'will' and more clearly contains ideas of wishing (*velle*), desire and intent. It would not be far wrong in this paragraph to think of *voluntas* and its derivatives as 'intention', 'intentional', etc.

30. **in quo et:** 'wherein they even..'

34. **prefati sumus:** see pp.4,6 of Luscombe's ed. *Hunc*

vero consensum proprie peccatum nominamus..Quid est enim iste consensus nisi Dei contemptus et offensa ipsius?..Peccatum itaque nostrum contemptus creatoris est.

47. **nequaquam tamen..nollemus:** 'yet we would not wish to be adulterous with her whom we would wish not to be married'. That is, we should prefer the intercourse without the adultery.

50. **potentum:** a Virgilian genitive plural?

53. **excedere:** 'transgress'; see L.& S. s.v. I B 2 a. The *magis* before *quam* is to be taken directly with the verb and *quam* = *potius quam*, as rarely in CL: 'to transgress more rather than less'.

63. **ille qui coactus:** see Luscombe's ed., pp.6,8. The man is pursued by his lord who has a drawn sword and intends to kill him; at last he is driven into a corner and *coactus tandem et nolens occidit eum ne occidatur ab eo.*

7. SAINT BONAVENTURE

Between Abelard and Bonaventure, indeed within sixty years or so of Abelard's death, medieval philosophy changed. In place of the restricted material at Abelard's disposal the 13th-century scholastic was able to work (at least in translation) with Aristotle's greater works - the *Analytics* , *Physics, Metaphysics, De Anima, Ethics* - and he was able to organise his work round the *Quattuor libri Sententiarum* of Peter Lombard. Although these introductory notes are not supposed to provide a 'potted' history of medieval philosophy, something must be said here about the Islamic philosophers Avicenna and Averroes, the Jew Maimonides, and Peter Lombard, the *Magister Sententiarum* .

Aristotle's works, in Greek, had been known to the Syrian Christians from the 5th to the 8th centuries, and from the latter half of the 8th century they had been translated into Arabic for the schools which began to flourish after the Muslem conquests of the eastern and southern Mediterranean and much of Spain. The Aristotelian corpus included however a *Theologia* derived from Plotinus' *Enneads* and the *Liber de Causis*, a compendium from the *Elements of Theology* of Proclus; so that Islamic Aristotelianism included many elements of Neoplatonism. Avicenna (Ibn Sina, 980-1037) wrote many works on logic, physics, metaphysics and psychology, in which he worked as a theologian fusing his Neoplatonist Aristotelianism with his Islamic theology. In the next century Averroes (Ibn Roshd, 1126-1198), known as 'the Commentator' for his commentaries on the works of Aristotle ('the Philosopher'), was perhaps as suspect to orthodox Islam for his extreme Aristotelianism as were his Latin followers (such as Siger of Brabant) to the Church in the next century. Averroes lived in Cordova, where his Jewish contemporary, Maimonides (Moses ben Maimon, 1135-1204), wrote his *Guide to the Perplexed*, which had some influence on Aquinas.

The influx of these writers' works, and of the pagan philosophy of Aristotle, in the late 12th century into the schools of Latin Christendom upset the Augustinian-Platonic tradition of thinking to such a degree that a statute of the new University of Paris in 1215 forbade the study of Aristotle's *Metaphysics*, while permitting the reading of the *Organon* ; and the study and teaching of Aristotle's philosophy was condemned by Pope Gregory IX in 1231, by Innocent IV in 1245, and by Urban IV in 1263. Prohibitions were however useless and the work of translation and study and commentary went on until in 1366 the study of Aristotle became compulsory in the schools. Broadly, all medieval philosophy after the mid-13th century is Aristotelian to some degree, but in various ways the Franciscans remained truer to the Augustinian tradition than did the Dominicans, who soon committed themselves to the purer Aristotelianism of Albertus Magnus and especially Thomas Aquinas.

Peter Lombard studied in Paris, where he probably heard Abelard teach, and after having studied in the school of St. Victor died in 1160 as Bishop of that same city. After 1152 he produced a compendium of 'The opinions of the Fathers' - *Patrum Sententiae* - in four books, the *Quattuor libri sententiarum*, culled from his own wide reading and from the *Glossa Ordinaria*, the collected commentary on the Scriptures. His first book dealt with God, the second with his creatures, the third with the Incarnation and the virtues, and the last with the sacraments and the Judgement. The sources that he used, besides Augustine, the chief authority, and the early Fathers, included Isidore, Bede and Boethius among the older writers, and Hugh of St. Victor, Ivo of Chartres and Abelard among the *moderni* ; he also quotes the *De fide orthodoxa* of John Damascene, which had been translated in 1151 by Burgundio of Pisa. So a full commentary on the Sentences covered the whole field of theology and much of philosophy, and some years of lecturing on Peter Lombard's collection of texts were later required before a man could proceed to his mastership and lecture on Holy Scripture. These preliminary years produced the *Commentarii in Sententias* and the *Breviloquium* of Bonaventure, from which our extracts are taken, is a kind of abridgement of his own commentary.

This commentary he wrote some time earlier than 1257, when he became Minister General of the Franciscan Order, which he had joined in about 1243. He was born about 1217 and studied in Paris, and after becoming a Franciscan he studied theology under Alexander of Hales, who, after long being regarded as a mere compiler, is now recognised as an important thinker in the Franciscan tradition. Bonaventure lectured on the Sentences and then on the Scriptures in the Franciscan Chair in Paris, where he succeeded John of Parma in 1248. After the Pope had intervened to settle the dispute between the secular professors and the regulars (secular clergy are those 'in the world' -

saeculum - and regular clergy those under a rule - *regula*) he became *magister regens* at the same time as his friend Thomas Aquinas, in 1257. At this time all members of Universities in France and England were clerks - *clerici*, clerics: the word originally meant 'chosen' - in at least minor orders, and hence under the discipline of the Church. The two 'regular' chairs of theology at Paris were filled by a Franciscan and a Dominican. The Dominicans, *Ordo Praedicatorum*, had been founded as a preaching, teaching order to combat heresy and to preach the Gospel in the areas of Southern France and of Spain reclaimed from Albigensians or Muslim. The Franciscans, the little brothers of St. Francis, *Ordo Fratrum Minorum*, were founded as an order of charity, of love: St. Francis was a mystic and moved by the love of Christ, whose *stigmata*, the marks of the Crucifixion, he bore. But one cannot preach love without words, and words involve argument, and the Franciscans soon found the need for learned brothers. In addition to Alexander of Hales and Bonaventure, the Order could boast the names of Robert Grosseteste, Roger Bacon, John Duns Scotus and William Ockham.

In 1265, at the age of about 47, Bonaventure might have been Archbishop of York, had he been compelled to accept Pope Clement IV's appointment. Instead, he continued as Minister General to the Franciscans. In 1273 he was made cardinal and appointed Papal Legate for the Council of Lyons, and after doing much of the organisational work necessary for the council he died on 15 July 1274. He was canonized in 1482.

In the first of these two extracts we consider the relations between philosophy and theology. The *Summa Theologica* of Aquinas begins with the question *utrum sit necessarium praeter philosophicas disciplinas aliam doctrinam haberi;* and the Prologue to Scotus' *Ordinatio* opens with the same question: *utrum homini pro statu isto sit necessarium aliquam doctrinam specialem supernaliter inspirari.* It was necessary to decide this question because there was a party in the schools that held that philosophy could provide all the answers. It was a question which would not, could not, have occurred to any Christian philosopher before the reception of Aristotle: that presented Christians with a whole philosophy that was entirely pagan. For the first time since Augustine almost, 'philosophy' meant something quite apart from Christianity. Hence Scotus makes it a dispute between *philosophos* and *theologos* . The answer given explicitly by Aquinas and Scotus is implicit in all Bonaventure's work, but in this passage of the *Breviloquium* he makes the distinction between philosophy and theology on the basis of a division of the ways things exist. Philosophy is allowed to deal with things as they exist in nature or as concepts in the mind, whether naturally acquired by abstraction from sense experience or *naturaliter insiti* - the eternal *a priori* truths of Augustine. The rest is for theology. This of course leaves the real problem unanswered. How far is it possible to discover the truths <u>necessary for salvation</u> from the knowledge of the natural world and the *conceptus naturaliter insiti* ? It may be worth quoting what Tillich says in his *Systematic Theology* (I, p.46): 'The theologians of the early Franciscan school were well aware of what today is called an "existential" relation to truth. For them theology was practical knowledge, based on a participation of the knowing subject in the spiritual realities, a touching and tasting (*tactus* and *gustus*) of that with which he deals. Alexander of Hales and Bonaventure were strictly "experiential" theologians. They dedicated much labour to an analysis of the nature of the especially religious experience as distinct from other forms of experience. Behind their endeavours stood the mystical-Augustinian principle of the immediate awareness of "being-itself", which is, at the same time, "truth-itself" (*esse ipsum - verum ipsum*)'.

The second extract is concerned with the Judaeo-Christian doctrine of the creation, a dogma which directly contradicts one of the universally accepted axioms of classical Greek philosophy: *ex nihilo nihil fit* . For the Christian says, with the Jew, 'and God said *fiat lux, et lux erat*". The doctrine that God made the world out of nothing by a simple creative act, and that everything other than God himself was made by him, implies that a distinction must be made between God as pure, necessary being and his creatures as contingent, dependent beings. At the time Bonaventure was writing the Aristotelian doctrine of the eternity of the world was popular in the university. *Audivi* , he says, in his *Collationes de decem praeceptis* (quoted by his Spanish editors, p.113, note 1), *audivi cum fui scholaris de Aristotele, quod ponit mundum aeternum, et cum audivi rationes et argumenta quae fiebant ad hoc, incepit concuti cor meum et incepi cogitare quomodo potest hoc esse? Sed haec modo sunt ita manifesta ut nullus de hoc possit dubitare.* This is the first *error qui repudiatur* ; for Bonaventure creation from nothing implies creation in time, since eternal creation would make the creature co-eternal with the creator. The second error is that of the Neoplatonists who followed the *Timaeus* with its account of the Demiurge fashioning the world in accordance with the Ideas as patterns from pre-existent matter. There was something of this, perhaps, in the school of Chartres and in Bernard Silvestris, and certainly it is part of the theories of the Manichees, whose evil, material principle was co-eternal - though perhaps not exactly equal - with the spiritual, good principle. The Neoplatonist idea of a *ministerium intelligentiarum* is discussed in the notes to the extract, as is the 'threefold causality', an idea showing a nice blending of Aristotle and his causes with Augustine and the *vestigia Dei* .

The doctrine of the creation and the problem of the relation between philosophy and theology are closely linked. The ideas of creator and created lead to the transcendence of God. Although it is possible to know God in his effects, in his creation, yet he is ultimate, eternal, infinite; we are contingent, bound by time and space and limited in countless ways in our action and in our understanding. Our finitude and our consciousness of our finitude demand revelation; and Christianity is essentially a revealed religion. But the problem at once arises, what is the relation of our finite reason to the infinite object of revelation? How far, if at all, can we know what has been revealed without revelation? Would it be possible to discover by using our reason the truths of God and our relation to him? It is at least suggested that we could by St. Paul in Romans 1,19-20: 'Because that which may be known of God is manifest in them (sc.the Gentiles); for God hath shewed it unto them. For the invisible things of him from the creation of the world are clearly seen, being understood by the things that are made, even his eternal power and godhead.' Bonaventure's answer to these questions is Franciscan, Augustinian, as is shown in the third and longest extract: without grace we know nothing, and understand nothing, because of sin. In a sense, the *Itinerarium mentis in Deum* is what Augustinian philosophy, Bonaventure's philosophy, is all about.

BIBLIOGRAPHY

Etienne Gilson's *The Philosophy of St. Bonaventure* , London 1948, should be read in conjunction with F. van Steenberghen's two books, *The Philosophical Movement in the Thirteenth Century* , Edinburgh 1955, and *Aristotle in the West* , Louvain 1955. There is a dauntingly large but excellent book by J.F. Quinn, *The Historical Constitution of St. Bonaventure's Philosophy* , Toronto 1973, which has a good introduction and index, as well as a full bibliography. The third volume of the five published for the seventh centenary of Bonaventure's death, edited by the Commissio Internationalis Bonaventuriana in 1973, is concerned with his philosophy.

1. Bonaventure: Theology and Philosophy

In Breviloquium Prologus § 3, Obras de San Buenaventura I, Madrid 1945.

Habet nihilominus sacra Scriptura in suo processu
sublimitatem, quae consistit in descriptione hierar-
3   chiarum gradatim ordinatarum, quae sunt hierarchia
ecclesiastica, angelica et divina seu subcaelestis, caelestis et supercaelestis; ita quod primam describit pat-
6   enter, secundam aliquantulum magis occulte et tertiam
adhuc magis occulte. Ex descriptione ecclesiasticae
hierarchiae est alta; ex descriptione angelicae altior;
9   ex descriptione divinae altissima, ita ut possimus dicere illud Prophetae: *mirabilis facta est scientia tua ex
me; confortata est, et non potero ad eam.*
12   Et hoc quidem satis recte. Nam cum res habeant
esse in materia, habeant esse in anima per notitiam
acquisitam, habeant etiam esse in ea per gratiam, hab-
15   eant esse in ea per gloriam et habeant esse in arte
aeterna; philosophia quidem agit de rebus, ut sunt in
natura, seu in anima secundum notitiam naturaliter in-
18   sitam, vel etiam acquisitam; sed theologia, tamquam
scientia supra fidem fundata et per Spiritum Sanctum
revelata, agit et de eis quae spectant ad gratiam et glo-
21   riam et etiam ad Sapientiam aeternam. Unde ipsa sub-
sternens sibi philosophicam cognitionem et assumens
de naturis rerum, quantum sibi opus est ad fabrican-
24   dum speculum, per quod fiat repraesentatio divinorum
quasi scalam erigit, quae in suo infimo tangit terram,
sed in suo cacumine tangit caelum; et hoc totum per
27   illum unum hierarcham, Iesum Christum, qui non tantum ratione naturae humanae assumptae est hierarcha
in ecclesiastica hierarchia, verum etiam in angelica, et
30   media persona in illa supercaelesti hierarchia beatissi-
mae Trinitatis; ita quod per ipsum a summo capite Deo
descendit unctionis gratia non solum in barbam verum
33   etiam in oram vestimenti,quia non tantum in Ierusalem
supernam verum etiam usque in Ecclesiam militantem.
Est enim pulchritudo magna in machina mundana,
36   sed longe maior in Ecclesia pulchritudine sanctorum

charismatum adornata, maxima autem in Ierusalem
superna, supermaxima autem in illa Trinitate summa
39 et beatissima. Ideo ipsa Scriptura non tantum habet
altissimam materiam, per quam delectat et per quam in
altum levat intelligentiam mentis, verum etiam ipsa est
42 venustissima et miro quodam modo intellectum nostrum delectat, et sic magis ac magis delectando assuefacit ad divinorum spectaculorum contuitus et anago-
45 gias.

Notes

1. **processu:** cf. Cic., *Brut.* 65,232: *processus
   dicendi,* 'mode of advancing', 'progress', implying
   here that the sublimity is not in any part but in the
   ordered unfolding of the whole.
2. **hierarchiarum:** the word is first used in 9th-c.trans-
   lations of Pseudo-Dionysius; it is simply a transliteration of the Greek word, itself first used by Pseudo-
   Dionysius it seems, though *hierarches* , 'high priest',
   is known from earlier inscriptions.
4. **subcaelestis:** quoted in L.& S. as occurring in Tertullian, *Adv.Val.* 31, though Kroyman in CSEL 47
   prints *caelesti* without noting any variants. *Supercaelestis* at any rate is as old as Tertullian, and its
   analogue is surely older than 13th or even 9th c., especially since its Greek, *hypouranios*, is as old as
   Homer and occurs in Plato (*Phaedrus* 247B).
5. **ita quod:** 'in such a way that'; with or without the
   subjunctive, this is common in 13th c. and later: cf.
   Ockham, *In Sent.* III,q.9 Q: *univocum accipitur uno
   modo pro concepto communi..ita quod hoc sit verum
   tam in substantialibus quam in accidentalibus, sic
   quod in forma accidentali non est reperiri* etc., where
   ita quod and *sic quod* both mean 'so that', and one is
   followed by the subjunctive and the other by the indicative.
7. **magis occulte:** in all periods of Latin, comparison
   with *magis, maxime* rather than by inflexion was
   possible, and in the early and late periods common.
   Donatus says on Ter., *Eun.*227: *animadverte ut amet*

Terentius magis addere quam comparativam facere;
and Servius on Virgil, *Aen*.IV,31: *antiqui frequenter
pro comparativo iungebant particulum magis*. The
preference for this form of comparison, partly
because of its simplicity and partly because of confusion of endings when slurred in pronunciation, is
shown in the Spanish comparative form *más* . Elsewhere in the Roman Empire the confusion between
magis and *plus,* and the development of *magis* (=
potius, 'rather') to 'but'(Fr. *mais,* It. *mai*) led to the
Romance comparison with *plus, più* .

9. **ex descriptione:** *ex* = 'by reason of' (L.& S. s.v.
   III E,1); 'fitting', 'suitable to' as in *ex usu* etc. and
   'for' in *ex utilitate* (Tacitus).

10. **illud Prophetae:** sc. *dictum;* for *Propheta* see note
    on line 10 of the first extract from Augustine.
    ex me: see note on *ex descriptione* above.

11. **confortata:** only in Christian Latin, esp. Vulgate,
    OT; lit. 'it has been made strong'.
    ad eam: either understand *adire* or some such infin-
    itive, or take *potero* absolutely, 'have power', and *ad*
    as meaning 'compared with'. The sense is much the
    same.

12. **nam cum res habeant esse:** things have being (a)
    in materia, e.g. men, tables and so on; (b) *in anima*
    (i) *per notitiam acquisitam,* e.g. the universals 'man',
    'table' etc.; (ii) *per gratiam* , e.g. the Trinity, and
    other revealed mysteries; (iii) *per gloriam,* the truths
    known in the full vision of God either in heaven or in
    mystical experience; and (c) *in arte aeterna,* the divine
    Ideas in the Logos. Philosophy deals with (a) and
    (b)(i), theology with the rest. Interesting points are
    raised by *notitiam naturaliter insitam vel etiam acqui-
    sitam* - is the knowledge of God's existence *natura-
    liter insita* ? - but they are not relevant to the distinc-
    tion made here between philosophy and theology.

18. **theologia:** transliterated from the Greek, and used,
    according to Augustine, *Civ.Dei,* VI,5, by Varro. It is
    common in 13th c.

22. **assumens etc:** cf. Romans I,20: *invisibilia Dei per*

ea quae facta sunt, intellecta conspiciuntur - a text often quoted in justification of natural theology and the study of the natural world.

25. **quasi scalam:** Genesis 28,12: *viditque in somnis scalam stantem super terram et cacumen illius tangens caelum.*

27. **hierarcham:** = Greek *hierarchen;* see note on line 2.

30. **ita quod:** see note on line 5.

31. **descendit unctionis gratia:** Ps. 132,1-2: *ecce quam bonum et quam iucundum, habitare fratres in unum. Sicut unguentum in capite, quod descendit in barbam, in barbam Aaron, quod descendit in oram vestimenti eius.*

34. **Ecclesiam militantem:** the old distinction should be familiar: the Church Suffering, the souls in Purgatory who will at last reach heaven; the Church Militant, engaged in the world with the fight against the devil; and the Church Triumphant, the saints in heaven.

35. **machina mundana:** 'the fabric of the world'; cf. Lucretius, V,96: *moles et machina mundi.*

37. **charismatum:** genitive plural; *charisma* = 'a gift of grace' (*charis*), common in all periods of Christian Latin.

42. **miro quodam modo:** not to be taken as *quidam* used 'to soften an assertion' (L.& S.) but 'to heighten the attribute by adding a vagueness to it', e.g. Cic., *Mil.* 37,101: *est quodam incredibili robore animi.*

43. **assuefacit:** sc. *eum = intellectum nostrum.*

44. **contuitus et anagogias:** *contuitus* = 'examination' from *contueor; anagogia,* transliterated from the Greek, is the higher, mystical interpretation of Scripture (the word means 'leading up'), and is a technical term of medieval exegesis, introduced by Jerome and John Cassian.

2. Bonaventure: The Creation
Breviloquium Part II, ch.1

His summatim praeintellectis de Trinitate Dei, dicenda
sunt aliqua de creatura mundi. Circa quam haec tenen-
3   da sunt in summa: videlicet quod universitas machinae
mundialis producta est in esse ex tempore et de nihilo
ab uno principio primo, solo et summo;cuius potentia,
6   licet sit immensa, disposuit tamen *omnia in certo pon-*
dere, numero et mensura.
Haec generaliter intelligenda sunt circa rerum pro-
9   ductionem, ex quibus veritas colligitur, et error repudiatur. Per hoc enim, quod dicitur ex tempore, excluditur error ponentium mundum aeternum. Per hoc,
12   quod dicitur de nihilo, excluditur error ponentium
aeternitatem circa principium materiale. Per hoc, quod
dicitur ab uno principio, excluditur error Manichae-
15   orum ponentium pluralitatem principiorum. Per hoc,
quod dicitur solo et summo, excluditur error ponentium, Deum produxisse inferiores creaturas per minis-
18   terium intelligentiarum. Per hoc autem, quod additur
in certo pondere, numero et mensura, ostenditur,
quod creatura est effectus Trinitatis creantis sub tri-
21   plici genere causalitatis: *efficientis,* a quo est in creatura unitas, modus et mensura; *exemplaris,* a quo est
in creatura veritas, species et numerus; *finalis,* a quo
24   est in creatura bonitas, ordo et pondus. Quae quidem
reperiuntur in omnibus creaturis tanquam vestigium
Creatoris sive corporalibus, sive spiritualibus, sive ex
27   utrisque compositis.
Ratio autem ad intelligentiam praedictorum haec est:
quia ad hoc, quod sit ordo perfectus et status in rebus,
30   necesse est, quod omnia reducantur ad unum principium, quod quidem sit primum, ut det ceteris statum;
et perfectissimum, ut det ceteris omnibus complemen-
33   tum. Quoniam igitur primum principium, in quo est
status, non potest esse nisi unum solum; si mundum
producit, cum non possit ipsum producere de se ipso,
36   necesse est, quod producat ex nihilo. Et quia productio ex nihilo ponit *esse* post *non-esse* ex parte pro-

ducti, et immensitatem in virtute producente ex parte
39 principii, cum hoc sit solius Dei, necesse est, quod
creatura mundi sit producta ex tempore ab ipsa virtute
immensa, agente per se et immediate.
42 Rursus, quoniam principium perfectissimum, a quo
manat perfectio universorum, necesse est agere a se et
secundum se et propter se - quia nullo in agendo indi-
45 get extra se - necesse est, quod habeat respectu cuius-
libet creaturae intentionem triplicis causae, scilicet
efficientis, exemplaris et finalis; necesse est etiam,
48 omnem creaturam secundum hanc triplicem habitudinem comparari ad causam primam. Omnis enim creatura constituitur in esse ab efficiente, conformatur ad
51 exemplar et ordinatur ad finem; ac per hoc est una,
vera, bona; modificata, speciosa, ordinata; mensurata,
discreta, et ponderata: est enim pondus inclinatio ordi-
54 nata. Et haec quidem generaliter dicta sunt de omni
creatura, sive corporea, sive incorporea, sive ex utrisque composita, sicut est natura humana.

Notes

1. **praeintellectis:** 'understood beforehand'; the word
is not found in CL, but occurs as early as Boethius as
a more exact term for CL *praenoscere* ; Boethius, *In
Isag.Porph. ed.* I,II,29: *huc accedit quod species
praenoscuntur, id est praeintelliguntur.*
3. **in summa:** CL generally *ad summam:* 'in a word'.
universitas: 'the whole of'; cf. Cic., *N.D.* II,65,
164: *universitas generis humani.*
4. **mundialis:** here equivalent to *mundanae* or the gen.
mundi , and not metaphorically 'mundane' as most
frequently. Cf. Tert., *Spect.* 9: *elementa mundialia.*
producta est: *producere* is so used, meaning 'to
beget', 'produce' infrequently in early and late CL: cf.
Seneca, *Ep. CIV,* 23: *magnanimos nos natura pro-
duxit.*
ex tempore: in CL means 'instantaneously', but
here it means 'in time', as in Chalcidius' 'translation'
of Plato's *Timaeus,* 28B: *item, mundus fueritne*

semper citra exordium temporis an sit originem sortitus ex tempore, considerandum.

6. **omnia in certo pondere:** Vulgate, Sap.11,21.

8. **productionem:** in CL only literally, 'drawn out', opposed to *contractio;* here = 'begetting', 'production'; cf. Boethius, *De Trin.* V,44: *substantialis est ei productio filii.*

15. **pluralitatem:** this word, and *pluralis,* the adjective from which it is derived, are both late words, the adj. first found in Quintilian and the noun in Ambrose and Boethius.

18. **intelligentiarum:** these are probably the *noes,* 'intelligences' of Proclus' *Elements of Theology,* a compilation from which, made in Arabic in the 9th c. and translated into Latin in the 12th c. by Gerard of Cremona, was known as the *Liber de Causis,* and attributed to Aristotle, though the truth of the matter was known to Aquinas. In the Neoplatonist scheme of emanation, adapted to theological needs by both Christians and Arabs, the intelligences performed an intermediate role between the first cause and the (created) things of this world. Cf. *Liber de Causis,* prop.9: *et causa quidem prima non est intelligentia, neque anima, neque natura, immo est supra intelligentiam, et animam et naturam, quoniam est creans omnes res: verumtamen est causans intelligentiam absque medio, et causans animam et naturam, et reliquas res, mediante intelligentia.*

21. **causalitatis:** TLL gives this as occurring in Ps.-Aug., *Quaest. Test.,* I,122, but the best MSS have a different reading (cf. Souter in CSEL 50); I have met no earlier occurrence of *causalitas* , (though *causalis* was probably a grammatical term and as old as the Latin grammarians) and it was probably introduced late in the 12th c. in connection with Aristotle's works.

efficientis **etc.:** Aristotle postulated, of course, <u>four</u> causes: efficient, formal, final, and material - the sculptor, the idea of the statue in his mind, the finished statue and the stone from which it is made.

The last is excluded from the creation by the doctrine that God created the world *ex nihilo,* so three causes are left, as is fitting when the agent is the Trinity.

26. ex utrisque compositis: sc.'man'; cf. line 56.

29. ad hoc, quod sit: cf. *necesse est, quod omnia reducantur* in the next line, where again *quod* has the sense of *ut;* it is easy to see how the uses of e.g. French *que* developed. The origins lie in such constructions as *magis est quod tibi gratuler quam etc.* Cic., *Att.* XVI, 5, 2, and *non est quod multa loquamur,* Hor., *Ep.* II,I,30.

31. quod quidem: this *quod* , on the other hand, is purely relative, and the *sit* a sort of jussive: 'which indeed has to be'.

32. complementum: a rare word used metaphorically in CL, but here literally 'that which makes them complete'.

41. immediate: 'with no intermediate agencies'; the adv. appears to be 13th-c. but the adj. *immediatus = sine medio,* is used by Boethius, *Cat.,* 279B (P.L.69): *immediata contraria..quae mediis carent.*

46. intentionem: 'application' and so 'relation to', derived from the idea 'attention to', itself from the literal meaning of 'straining towards'.

48. habitudinem: 'condition', used in early and late Latin, while CL writers preferred *habitus.*

3. Bonaventure: The Ascent to God
Itinerarium mentis in Deum, ch.1

*Beatus vir, cuius est auxilium abs te, ascensiones in
corde suo disposuit in valle lacrymarum, in loco,*
3 *quem posuit.* Cum beatitudo nihil aliud sit, quam
summi boni fruitio; et summum bonum sit supra nos:
nullus potest effici beatus, nisi supra semetipsum as-
6 cendat, non ascensu corporali, sed cordiali. Sed supra
nos levari non possumus nisi per virtutem superiorem
nos elevantem. Quantumcumque enim gradus interio-
9 res disponantur, nihil fit, nisi divinum auxilium comi-
tetur. Divinum autem auxilium comitatur eos qui
petunt ex corde humiliter et devote;et hoc est ad ipsum
12 suspirare in hac lacrymarum valle, quod fit per fer-
ventem orationem. Oratio igitur est mater et origo
sursum-actionis. Ideo Dionysius in libro *De Mystica*
15 *Theologia,* volens nos instruere ad excessus mentales,
primo praemittit orationem. Oremus igitur et dicamus
ad Dominum Deum nostrum: *Deduc me, Domine, in*
18 *via tua, et ingrediar in veritate tua; laetetur cor meum,*
ut timeat nomen tuum.
   In hac oratione orando illuminamur ad cognoscen-
21 dum divinae ascensionis gradus. Cum enim secundum statum conditionis nostrae ipsa rerum universitas sit scala ad ascendum in Deum; et in rebus quae-
24 dam sint vestigium, quaedam imago, quaedam corporalia, quaedam spiritualia, quaedam temporalia, quaedam aeviterna; ac per hoc quod perveniamus ad
27 primum principium considerandum, quod est spiritu-
alissimum et aeternum et supra nos, oportet nos trans-
ire per vestigium, quod est corporale et temporale et
30 extra nos, et hoc est deduci in via Dei; oportet nos in-
trare ad mentem nostram quae est imago Dei aeviterna, spiritualis et intra nos, et hoc est ingredi in ver-
33 itate Dei; oportet nos transcendere ad aeternum, spiri-
tualissimum, et supra nos aspiciendo ad primum principium, et hoc est laetari in Dei notitia et reverentia
36 Maiestatis.
   Haec est igitur via trium dierum in solitudine; haec

est triplex illuminatio unius diei, et prima est sicut
39 vespera, secunda est sicut mane, tertia sicut meridies;
haec respicit triplicem rerum existentiam, scilicet in
materia, in intelligentia et in arte aeterna, secundum
42 quod dictum est, *fiat, fecit et factum est* ; haec etiam
respicit triplicem substantiam in Christo, qui est scala
nostra, scilicet corporalem, spiritualem et divinam.
45   Secundum hunc triplicem progressum mens nostra
tres habet aspectus principales. Unus est ad corporalia
exteriora, secundum quem vocatur animalitas seu sen-
48 sualitas; alius intra se et in se, secundum quem dicitur
spiritus; tertius supra se, secundum quem dicitur
mens. Ex quibus omnibus disponere se debet ad con-
51 scendendum in Deum, ut ipsum diligat *ex tota mente,*
ex toto corde et ex tota anima, in quo consistit perfecta
Legis observatio et simul cum hoc sapientia christi-
54 ana.
       Quoniam autem quilibet praedictorum modorum ge-
minatur, secundum quod contingit considerare Deum
57 ut *alpha et omega,* seu in quantum contingit videre
Deum in unoquoque praedictorum modorum ut *per*
speculum et ut *in speculo,* seu quia una istarum con-
60 siderationum habet commisceri alteri sibi coniunctae et
habet considerari in sua puritate; hinc est, quod necesse est, hos tres gradus principales ascendere ad sen-
63 arium, ut, sicut Deus sex diebus perfecit universum
mundum et in septimo requievit; sic minor mundus
sex gradibus illuminationum sibi succedentium ad
66 quietem contemplationis ordinatissime perducatur. In
cuius rei figura sex gradibus ascendebatur ad thronum
Salomonis; Seraphim, quae vidit Isaias, senas alas
69 habebant; post sex dies *vocavit* Dominus *Moysen de*
medio caliginis et Christus *post sex dies,* ut dicitur
Matthaeo, *duxit discipulos in montem et transfigur-*
72 *atus est ante eos.*
       Iuxta igitur sex gradus ascensionis in Deum sex
sunt gradus potentiarum animae per quos ascendimus
75 ab imis ad summa, ab exterioribus ad intima, a temp-
oralibus conscendimus ad aeterna, scilicet sensus,
imaginatio, ratio, intellectus, intelligentia et apex

78 mentis seu synderesis scintilla. Hos gradus in nobis
habemus plantatos per naturam, deformatos per culpam, reformatos per gratiam; purgandos per iustitiam,
81 exercendos per scientiam, perficiendos per sapientiam.
    Secundum enim primam naturae institutionem crea-
84 tus fuit homo habilis ad contemplationis quietem, et
ideo *posuit eum Deus in paradiso deliciarum* . Sed
avertens se a vero lumine ad commutabile bonum, in-
87 curvatus est ipse per culpam propriam, et totum genus
suum per originale peccatum, quod dupliciter infecit
humanam naturam, scilicet ignorantia mentem, et con-
90 cupiscentia carnem; ita quod excaecatus homo et in-
curvatus in tenebris sedet et caeli lumen non videt nisi
succurrat gratia cum iustitia contra concupiscentiam,
93 et scientia cum sapientia contra ignorantiam. Quod
totum fit per Iesum Christum, *qui factus est nobis a
Deo sapientia et iustitia et sanctificatio et redemptio.*
96 Qui cum sit Dei virtus et Dei sapientia, sit Verbum
incarnatum *plenum gratiae et veritatis,* gratiam et
veritatem fecit, gratiam scilicet caritatis infudit, quae
99 cum sit *de corde puro et conscientia bona et fide non
ficta,* totam animam rectificat secundum triplicem
ipsius aspectum supradictum; scientiam veritatis
102 edocuit secundum triplicem modum theologiae,
scilicet symbolicae, propriae et mysticae, ut per
symbolicam recte utamur sensibilibus, per propriam
105 recte utamur intelligibilibus, per mysticam rapiamur
ad supermentales excessus.
    Qui igitur vult in Deum ascendere necesse est ut
108 vitata culpa deformante naturam, naturales potentias
supradictas exerceat ad gratiam reformantem, et hoc
per orationem; ad iustitiam purificantem et hoc in con-
111 versatione; ad scientiam illuminantem et hoc in medi-
tatione; ad sapientiam perficientem et hoc in contemplatione. Sicut igitur ad sapientiam nemo venit nisi per
114 gratiam, iustitiam et scientiam; sic ad contemplationem
non venitur nisi per meditationem perspicuam, con-
versationem sanctam et orationem devotam. Sicut
117 igitur gratia fundamentum est rectitudinis voluntatis et

illustrationis perspicuae rationis; sic primo orandum
est nobis, deinde sancte vivendum, tertio veritatis
120 spectaculis intendendum et intendendo gradatim as-
cendendum, quousque veniatur ad montem excelsum,
ubi *videatur Deus deorum in Sion.*

Notes

1. *Beatus vir..:* Ps. 83,6-7; from older editions of the
Vulgate, with the Psalms in the Old Latin version,
derived from the Greek of the Septuagint. It does not
make much sense; the Douay version translates it
more or less literally:'Blessed is the man whose help
is from thee; in his heart he hath disposed to ascend
by steps, in the vale of tears, in the place which he
hath set'.

4. **fruitio:** a Christian writer's word, from 4th c. on.

6. **cordiali:** this word must surely have been coined
before the 13th c. - du Cange gives only 14th-c.
examples - but no dictionary helps. The CL adjective
is *cardiacus.*

11. **humiliter:** it is worth noting that *humilis, humilitas,*
etc., are 'bad' words in CL ('base','low','mean'),
but 'good' in Christian Latin; humility is a Judaeo-
Christian virtue, not a Classical one.
ad ipsum suspirare: in CL *suspirare* is used with
in and the ablative or a simple accusative; there may
be here some influence in Bonaventure's mind and
intention from *aspirare.*

14. **sursum-actionis:** so printed by the editors, but
Bonaventure uses as single words *sursumactio,
sursumactivus* often enough for them to be so regarded and so printed.
Dionysius: the 'Areopagite'; see Intro. to Erigena.

15. **excessus mentales:** cf. Acts 11,5, where Peter
describes his vision in Joppa 'in a trance' - the Greek
has *ekstasis,* and the Vulgate *in excessu mentis;* so
excessus mentales means ecstasies, in the technical
mystical meaning of the word.

16. **dicamus ad Dominum:** common in the Vulgate as

a translation of *eipein pros tina,* and reflecting also a very ancient mingling of the dative and *ad* + accus.

20. ad cognoscendum..gradus: the ancient use of the gerund with a direct object which almost disappeared (vulgar?) in CL, becomes common in late and medieval Latin.

24. vestigium..imago: with both supply *Dei* or *Creatoris.*

26. aeviterna: Priscian, quoting Varro, gives this as the ancient form for *aeternus.*Augustine and others affect it from time to time.

per hoc quod: 'for this, that we may arrive', where the *quod* is like that in *ita quod,* 'in such a way that', and both ='so that', the one being final, the other consecutive.

34. supra nos: not adverbially with *aspiciendo,* but substantivally as in line 28.

37. trium dierum in solitudine: cf. Exodus 3,18 and Moses' meeting with God in the burning bush.

38. unius diei: the day, like that of the Jews, began at sunset, so that the divisions are evening, morning, afternoon.

39. meridies: commonly opposed to morning, evening and night, and here = 'afternoon'.

40. respicit: 'has reference to'; cf. Oxford Latin Dictionary s.v., 9a (Quintilian).

42. *fiat, fecit et factum est:* cf. Genesis 1.

46. aspectus: in the active sense, meaning something like 'modes of perception' (cf. *modorum* in line 55). The subject of *vocatur* in line 47 is *mens nostra,* which is still one, not divided into three 'parts'.

47. sensualitas: here active; see note on line 30 of the first Abelard extract.

50. mens: clearly in line 45 its meaning is 'mind' in the broadest sense, corresponding to the Greek *psyche,* and here it perhaps means 'intellect', corresponding to *nous;* the first is L.& S. I, the second II B. The Spanish translators cheat a little, but rightly, using *alma* for the first and *mente* for the second.

51. *ex tota mente* etc.: Mk. 12,30.

53. simul cum hoc: if *hoc* is right, it must refer to *in quo*, i.e. *ipsum diligat..tota anima.*

58. *per speculum:* the two 'mirrors' are the external one, *per quem vidimus Deum,* the created world, and the internal one, the soul, *in quo vidimus eum.*

60. habet commisceri: *habet = potest;* cf. L.& S.II A 2

67. ascendebatur ad thronum Salomonis: I Kings 10,19. The other references in this paragraph are to Isaiah 6,2; Exodus 24,16; Mt.17,1ff.

78. synderesis scintilla: 'the spark of conscience'; *synderesis* is the medieval Latin representation of the actual pronunciation of the Greek *synteresis.* Jerome describes *synderesis* as *scintilla conscientiae.*

85. *posuit eum:* Genesis 2,15; the Old Latin versions from the Septuagint have *deliciarum;* Jerome's Vulgate, from the Hebrew, *voluptatis.*

94. *qui factus est:* I Cor. 1,30. The next two quotes are from John 1,14 and I Tim.1,5. *Iustitia* in a Christian theological context means 'righteousness' or some such, not 'justice'.

106 supermentales excessus: cf. note on line 15. *Supermentalis* must be from Erigena or another translator of Pseudo-Dionysius.

110 conversatione: see note on line 94 of the Benedict extract. Here it means generally 'way of life' not necessarily in a monastery or under a rule.

118 illustrationis: here = *illuminationis,* actively, meaning 'enlightenment' in the active, transitive sense with *rationis* as objective genitive. It appears to be a 4th-c. Christian word.

120 intendendum: clearly here equivalent to *meditandum,* and used with the dative (partly fairly naturally in that sense, and partly because of the confusion between the dative and *ad* + accus.). Such a use of *intendere* may already be evident in Seneca, *Q.N.* pr.1: *quid sit Deus: totus in se intendat, an ad nos aliquando aspiciat* (if the 12th-c.MSS are correct; modern editors print *tendat.*

122 *videatur Deus deorum in Sion:* Ps. 83,8 in the Old Latin version.

8. SAINT THOMAS AQUINAS

Next to Augustine Aquinas is surely the best known of all the philosophers of the Middle Ages, and most people have some idea of when he lived and what he did. His life is easily summarised. He was born at Roccasecca, near Monte Cassino and Naples, in 1225 and educated by the Benedictines of Monte Cassino and by the Dominicans of Naples, where he joined the Order of Preachers in 1243. In the following year he was sent to Cologne to study under Albertus Magnus, a man of encyclopaedic learning. From 1252 to 1256 he studied and taught in Paris before becoming Dominican Professor of Theology there in 1257. Two years later he joined the Papal Court of Urban IV, where he met William of Moerbeke, who in the years that followed assisted him with translations of and help in interpreting the Greek texts he needed. In 1269 he returned for three years to Paris and then taught for the last year or so of his life at the new University of Naples. He died at Fossanuova on his way to the Council of Lyons on 7 March 1274. Aquinas produced a vast number of philosophical, theological, exegetical and liturgical works, of which the best known are the Commentaries on the *Sentences*, the *Summa contra Gentiles*, and the unfinished *Summa Theologica*. The *Doctor angelicus*, or *Doctor communis*, as he was called, was canonised in 1323.

It was the main object of his work to effect a synthesis of Christian theology and Aristotle's philosophy. This was not done without opposition, not only, as was to be expected, from among the Franciscans, who were broadly Augustinian-Platonist in sympathy and later produced Aquinas' two greatest medieval critics, Scotus and Ockham, but also among the Dominicans, notably in the person of Robert Kilwardby, Oxford professor and then Archbishop and Cardinal. After St. Thomas's canonisation, however, his authority gradually increased and went on increasing until his philosophy became for centuries 'official' in the Roman Catholic Church. From the 14th century until today men have attacked him, defended him and argued over his teaching, and it is noticeable that the grounds for attack are very varied: Tillich accuses him of confounding theology and philosophy, Charles Raven held that he too dogmatically and disastrously separated them. But all, friend and opponent, have been agreed on the breadth and depth of his mind, and on his sanctity. In reading Aquinas one is struck at once by the firmness of the faith on which the massive intellect stands and which lends authority to his voice, and by the humility of the man. In this combination of authority and humility he was like many of the great saints, especially St. Augustine, and one also with his Master, for the Feast of whose Body (Corpus Christi) he composed so beautiful an office.

In taking over Aristotle's metaphysics Aquinas accepted the distinction between potency and act, and this may indeed be said to be the basis not only of Thomist metaphysics but of all his philosophy. Things may exist either in potency or in act and something only potential can only be brought into actuality by something already existing in act. From this distinction is derived that between matter and form and also between *esse* and *essentia*, which is relevant to the first two extracts. Your *esse* is yours, particular to you, it is your 'being', which makes actual your own *essentia*, which is the total of all your possible (not actual) perfections. Your *essentia*, being potency, possibility, is actualised by your *esse*, by your being, which is act. So *esse* and *essentia* are different in you and in all creatures. But they are not different in God. His Being is his essence. The two extracts from the *Summa contra Gentiles* - which, being written for the use of the Dominicans in the lands of southern France and of Spain reclaimed from heretics and Muslim, is more explicitly philosophical than the *Summa Theologiae* - are concerned with this matter: that God is his essence and that all else is from him. Whatever the metaphysical disagreements with Aquinas (and Aristotle), the Christian philosopher must reckon with the simplicity of the opening words of Genesis:'In the beginning God created..', and the Voice of Exodus 3,14:'I am WHO AM'. Whatever that means or meant, the distinction must be maintained between a creation entirely dependent for its coming into being and its continuing so on the will of the Creator, and the Creator as an absolutely necessary and transcendent being, God.

The third extract is included for several reasons. First, it illustrates a method; second, it introduces medieval science and its relations with inspired Scriptures; and third, it shows Aquinas on a plane a little lower than that of the great summas. He was a professor in Paris and Naples. One of the functions of a professor was to dispute, to argue questions, *quaestiones*. *Quaestiones disputatae* were regularly discussed, and organised by the Master as part of his course. Twice a year, on the eves of Easter and Christmas, he would dispute *quaestiones quodlibetales*, which were open to all, other masters and students alike, and anything at all might be asked: *cuilibet auditori fas erat quaestiones proponere, obiectiones movere* (Spiazzi, p.VII). So Aquinas' deal with God, angels, man and the world. For instance, Quodlibetum III, which dates from Easter 1270 in Paris, contains thirteen other questions beside the one used here, totalling thirty 'articles' ranging from 'whether God could make something material without form' through angels' influence on man, the duties of religious and the fallability of conscience, to 'whether it might be demonstrably proven that the world is not eternal' - to which Aquinas' answer is 'no': *creatio autem mundi non dependet ex alia causa nisi ex sola dei voluntate; unde ea quae ad principium mundi pertinent demonstrative probari non possunt, sed sola fide tenentur prophetice per Spiritum Sanctum revelata.* The method of procedure in these disputations is shown in the way in which they were published: the question is asked - *quaesitum est, quaerebatur utrum..*; the contrary or contradictory proposition to the thesis is set out - *videtur, videbatur quod non..*; and arguments and authorities cited. Then contrary authority is quoted - *sed contra..*; and there follows the *solutio*, the *responsio principalis - respondeo, dicendum..*; the body of the article. Lastly, the previous objections are answered - *ad primum..; ad secundum..*etc.(Spiazzi pp.XI-XII). The importance of these disputations and their place in the life of the medieval university are described by Spiazzi (p.XIII) as follows: 'There were as yet no newspapers, no news broadcasts. Accounts of actual and historic events seethed around the chairs of the universities, especially on the occasions of disputations *de quolibet. Quaestiones* were not the idle gossip of street-corner chatterers, but the inquiries of minds seeking truth; those disputing were not empty-headed and simple observers of the passing scene but noble minds, endowed with great powers of reasoning, skilled in the art of logic, and therefore fitted with exactly the tools to grasp the living truth of things about them. What today is investigated in modern ways, for example in the free arguments at Hyde Park, in radio and TV discussions, in society meetings and the like, was then inquired into in the courts of the universities, and especially in the *quaestiones quodlibetales*. We mean: *quodlibetum* means 'whatever you like', not implying red-herrings or arguing for the fun of it, but the inquiry into and discussion of and discovery of the truth, in all those difficult questions which troubled the minds of that time'.

Medieval science is too large and separate a subject for this book, but it cannot be ignored in any approach to the 13th and 14th centuries. Between the late 11th and early 12th-c. revival first of Greek medicine then of the rest of Greek mathematics and science, including *astrologia*, which comprised both astronomy and astrology, and the interesting early 14th-c. physicists and mathematicians, especially at Oxford, lie 300 years of extraordinary development, the story of which has only begun to emerge in the last thirty years or so, and has yet to be written. In the Middle Ages, a time when men believed in the wholeness, the oneness - and the accessibility - of truth, and also in the inspiration and therefore the multi-level interpretation of Scripture, there was not often occasion for argument between 'science' and 'religion'. And even with regard to a later period, those concerned with the 'Galileo affair' might reflect that Mersenne and Gassendi, who had much to do with the rise of 'modern science', were both Catholic priests. Our extract concerns an obvious enough problem for anyone taking Genesis 9,13 seriously. As to the physical cause of the rainbow, Aristotle and Seneca both explain it in terms of reflection; the Polish scholar Witelo, a contemporary of Aquinas, held that it was formed by refraction, and the Dominican Theoderic of Vriberg got it more or less right. It is not properly described until the 17th c. What perhaps strikes one most in the quodlibets of St. Thomas is his great common sense; *Doctor communis* was a good title.

BIBLIOGRAPHY

There are three good short general works on Aquinas: in chronological order they are F.C. Copleston *Aquinas*, Harmondsworth 1955, J. Weisheipl, *Friar Thomas d'Aquino*, Oxford 1974, A. Kenny, *Aquinas*, Oxford 1980. *Toward Understanding St. Thomas*, by M-D. Chenu, translated by A-M. Landry and D. Hughes, Chicago 1964 has a good bibliography; it is, of course, Dominican.

1. Aquinas: God's essence and existence
Summa contra Gentiles I, xxii, ed. Marietti, Turin 1927

Ex his autem, quae supra ostensa sunt, ulterius probari potest, quod in Deo non est aliud essentia vel
3   quidditas, quam suum esse.
Ostensum est supra (cap.xv) aliquid esse, quod per
se necesse est esse; quod Deus est. Hoc igitur esse,
6   quod necesse est, si est alicui quidditati coniunctum,
quae non est quod ipsum est, aut est dissonum illi
quidditati seu repugnans, sicut per se existere quid-
9   ditati albedinis; aut ei consonum sive affine, sicut
albedini esse in alio. Si primo modo, illi quidditati
non conveniet esse quod est per se necesse esse, sicut
12   nec albedini per se existere. Si autem secundo modo,
oportet quod vel esse huiusmodi dependeat ab essentia, vel utrumque ab alia causa, vel essentia ab esse.
15   Prima duo sunt contra rationem eius, quod est per se
necesse esse; quia, si ab alio dependet, iam non est
necesse esse. Ex tertio vero sequitur, quod illa quid-
18   ditas accidentaliter advenit ad eam rem quae per se
necesse est esse; quia omne quod sequitur ad esse rei,
est ei accidentale: et sic non erit eius quidditas. Deus
21   igitur non habet essentiam, quae non sit suum esse.
Sed contra hoc potest dici quod illum esse non absolute dependet ab essentia illa, ut omnino non sit,
24   nisi illa esset; sed dependet quantum ad coniunctio-
nem, qua ei coniungitur; et sic illud esse per se necesse est, sed ipsum coniungi non per se necesse est.
27   Haec autem responsio praedicta inconvenientia non
evadit, quia si illud esse potest intelligi sine illa essentia, sequitur quod illa essentia accidentaliter se habet
30   ad illud esse; sed id quod est per se, necesse est illud
esse. Ergo illa essentia se habet accidentaliter ad id,
quod est per se necesse esse; non ergo est quidditas
33   eius. Hoc autem, quod est per se necesse esse, est
Deus. Non igitur illa est essentia Dei, sed aliqua essentia Deo posterior. Si autem non potest intelligi illud
36   esse sine illa essentia, tunc illud esse absolute dependet ab eo, a quo dependet coniunctio sua ad essentiam

illam; et sic redit idem quod prius.

39   Item, unumquodque est per suum esse. Quod igitur
non est suum esse non est per se necesse esse. Deus
autem est per se necesse esse; ergo Deus est suum
42   esse.
        Amplius, omnis res est per hoc quod habet esse;
nulla igitur res, cuius essentia non est suum esse, est
45   per essentiam suam, sed participatione alicuius, scilicet ipsius esse. Quod autem est per participationem
alicuius non potest esse primum ens; quia id, quo ali-
48   quid participat ad hoc quod sit, est eo prius. Deus.
autem est primum ens, quo nihil est prius. Dei igitur
essentia est suum esse.
51   Hanc autem sublimem veritatem Moyses a Domino
est edoctus, qui, quum quaereret a Domino, dicens: *Si
dixerint ad me filii Israel: quod est nomen eius; quid*
54   *dicam eis?* Dominus respondit: *ego sum qui sum; sic
dices filiis Israel: Qui est, misit me ad vos* (Exodus 3,
13-14), ostendens suum proprium nomen esse: *Qui*
57   *est.* Quodlibet autem nomen est institutum ad significandum naturam seu essentiam alicuius rei. Unde
relinquitur quod ipsum divinum esse est sua essentia
60   vel natura. Hanc etiam veritatem catholici doctores
professi sunt. Ait namque Hilarius in libro de Trinitate
(VII, init.): *esse non accidens Deo, sed subsistens*
63   *veritas, et manens causa, et naturalis generis proprie-
tas.* Boethius etiam dicit in libro de Trinitate (c.2)
quod *divina substantia est ipsum esse, et ab ea est*
66   *esse.*

Notes

3. quidditas: 'whatness', the answer to 'What's that?'
The word, formed on the somewhat stretched analogy
of *qualitas, quantitas,* occurs in the *Liber de Praedica-
bilibus* of Albertus Magnus, tract.1, c.5 (ed.Vives
p.8): *istae ergo sunt duae partes logicae, una quidem
ut doceantur principia per quae sciatur definitio rei et
quidditatis, ita quod* etc. It was probably another
coinage of the 13th-c. schools or the translators.

4. **per se necesse est esse:** it would be difficult to construe the various uses of *necesse* in this passage; certainly all the following are equivalent: *per se necesse esse, quod necesse est, quod est per se* - all mean 'necessary being', i.e. God.

10. **albedini:** dative with *consonum sive affine; esse in alio* is what is consistent with or akin to whiteness.

13. **oportet quod..dependeat:** *oportere ut* is used by Augustine and Boethius, and is common in LL, and we have had many examples of *quod = ut*. *Dependere,* 'to depend on (hang from)', is usually construed with *ex* in CL.

18. **accidentaliter:** a technical philosophical term introduced by Boethius, *In Isag.Porph.,* ed.II,iv,17: *quae de aliquo praedicantur, vel substantialiter vel accidentaliter dicuntur.* In 'Jones is a white man', 'man' is predicated *substantialiter,* as to be a man is of Jones' substance, but 'white' is predicated *accidentaliter,* as whiteness is an 'accident', Jones happens to be (*accidit ut*) white - he could be black without ceasing to be a man and Jones.
advenit: probably perfect rather than present:'is present with (has been added to)'; for the meaning cf. Lucr. 3,825: *advenit id, quod..*'this is added, that..'.

19. **sequitur ad:** the *ad* is simply 'in respect to' (cf. line 29), but it may be a development of *ad* + accus. for dative, as *sequor* takes a dative in LL, possibly in imitation of the equivalent Greek verb.

21. **quae non sit suum esse:** the subjunctive is consecutive:'which is such as not to be his being'.Clearly a negative antecedent often logically produces such a subjunctive.

27. **inconvenientia:** 'inconsistency', 'contradiction': cf. Tert.*Adv.Marc.* 4,16: *denique hac inconvenientia voluntatis et facti agunt ethnici nondum a Deo instructi.*

29. **se habet ad:** *ad* ='with respect to'; for *se habere* see L.& S. s.v. II B 6.

37. **coniunctio sua ad:** cf. 'joined to' and 'joined with'. The dative is used with the verb in line 25, and see note on line 19 for the confusion of *ad* + accus. with the dative.

39. Item, unumquodque etc: the validity of this syllogism can be more easily seen if the major is simply converted and the negatives cancelled: instead of *quod..non est suum esse non est per se necesse esse,* by conversion we have *nihil quod est per se necesse esse non est suum esse,* and since *nihil..non = omne,* we get *omne quod est per se necesse esse est suum esse;* taking that as the major, and *Deus autem est per se necesse esse* as the minor, the conclusion is *ergo Deus est suum esse.*

52. qui, quum quaereret a Domino, dicens.. Dominus respondit: anacoluthon, unless *qui* should be *cui,* and was attracted into the nominative by the (actually invariant) *dicens.*

53. dixerint ad me: surely exactly *dixerint mihi.* *quod est nomen eius:* Kühner says, after remarking that *quis* and *qui* are sometimes confused, that *quid* and *quod* are always strictly distinguished. There are however many instances of the interrogative pronoun *quod* in Patristic and late Latin, e.g. Aug., *In Iohann.Evang.*II,16,5: *ideo factum est Verbum caro, et habitavit in nobis. Sanavit oculos nostros. Et quod sequitur? Et vidimus gloriam eius.* The ambiguity might be partly due to the Hebrew, since there the pronoun is both interrogative and indefinite, and 'is sometimes followed by a substantive in apposition so that it becomes virtually an adjective' (Gesenius Lexicon), but confusion of *quid* and *quod* is common in all periods of LL.

57. quodlibet autem nomen: cf. Priscian II,22: *nomen quasi notamen, quod hoc notamus uniuscuiusque substantiae qualitatem.*

2. Aquinas: Everything is from God
Summa contra Gentiles, II, xv.

Quia vero ostensum est quod Deus est aliquibus essendi principium, oportet ulterius ostendere quod nihil
3 praeter ipsum est nisi ab ipso.
   Omne enim quod alicui convenit non secundum
quod ipsum est, per aliquam causam convenit ei, sicut
6 album homini; nam quod causam non habet, primum
et immediatum est; unde necesse est quod sit per se et
secundum quod ipsum. Impossibile est autem aliquod
9 unum duobus convenire, et utrique secundum quod
ipsum; quod enim de aliquo secundum quod ipsum
dicitur, ipsum non excedit; sicut habere tres angulos
12 duobus rectis aequales non excedit triangulum de quo
praedicatur, sed est eidem convertibile. Si igitur aliquid duobus conveniat, non convenit utrique secun-
15 dum quod ipsum est. Impossibile est igitur aliquod
unum de duobus praedicari, ita quod de neutro per
causam dicatur; sed oportet vel unum esse alterius
18 causa, sicut ignis est causa caloris corpori mixto, cum
tamen utrumque calidum dicatur; vel oportet quod aliquod tertium sit causa utrique, sicut duabus candelis
21 ignis est causa lucendi. Esse autem dicitur de omni eo
quod est. Impossibile est igitur esse aliqua duo, quorum neutrum habeat causam essendi, sed oportet
24 utrumque acceptorum esse per causam, vel alterum
alteri esse causam essendi. Oportet igitur quod ab illo
cui nihil est causa essendi sit omne illud quod quo-
27 cumque modo est. Deum autem supra (I, xiii) ostendimus huiusmodi ens esse cui nihil sit causa essendi.
Ab eo igitur est omne quod quocumque modo est. Si
30 autem dicatur quod ens non est praedicatum univocum
nihilominus praedicta conclusio sequetur; non enim de
multis aequivoce dicitur, sed per analogiam; et sic
33 oportet fieri reductionem in unum.
   Amplius, quod alicui convenit ex sua natura et non
ex aliqua causa, minoratum in eo et deficiens esse non
36 potest. Si enim naturae aliquid essentiale subtrahitur
vel additur, iam altera natura erit; sicut et in numeris

39 accidit, in quibus unitas addita vel subtracta species
variat. Si autem, natura vel quidditate rei integra man-
ente, aliquid minoratum inveniatur, iam patet quod
illud non simpliciter dependet ex illa natura, sed ex
42 aliqua alia causa per cuius remotionem minoratur.
Quod igitur alicui minus convenit quam aliis, non
convenit ei ex sua natura tantum, sed ex alia causa.
45 Illud igitur erit causa omnium in aliquo genere, cui
maxime convenit illius generis praedicatio; unde etiam
quod maxime calidum est, videmus esse causam calo-
48 ris in omnibus calidis, et quod maxime lucidum est,
causa omnium lucidorum. Deus autem est maxime
ens, ut ostensum est. Ipse igitur est causa omnium de
51 quibus ens praedicatur.
Amplius, Deus secundum hoc factivus est rerum
quod actu est, ut supra ostensum est. Ipse autem sua
54 actualitate et perfectione omnes rerum perfectiones
comprehendit, ut probatum est(I, xxviii); et sic est virtualiter omnia. Est igitur ipse omnium factivus. Hoc
57 autem non esset, si aliquid aliud esset natum esse nisi
ab ipso; nihil enim natum est esse ab alio et esse non
ab alio, quia si natum est non ab alio esse, est per se-
60 ipsum necesse esse; quod non potest ab alio esse.
Nihil igitur potest esse nisi a Deo.
Hoc autem divina confirmat auctoritas.Dicitur enim:
63 *qui fecit caelum et terram, mare, et omnia quae in eis*
sunt (Ps.145,6); et: *omnia per ipsum facta sunt, et*
sine ipso factum est nihil (John 1,3); et: *ex quo*
66 *omnia, per quem omnia, et in quo omnia. Ipsi gloria*
in saecula (Rom. 11,36).

Notes

1. **essendi:** the gerund of *esse* ; cf. Aug., *Ars Gramm.*
   breviata (Keil, V,494-95): *sed docti quidam temporis*
   recentioris..et essendi et essendo et essendum et ess-
   ens dixerunt, quemadmodum scribendi etc. The word
   is freely used by Erigena.
4. **secundum quod ipsum est:** e.g. *rationalitas con-*
   venit homini secundum quod homo est.

11. **ipsum non excedit:** that is, exceed (go beyond) it as defined, go beyond the definition. 'Having three angles together equal to two right angles' is part of the nature, the definition, of a plane triangle, so this predicate (*quod de triangulo secundum quod ipsum dicitur*) does not go beyond (*non excedit*) 'triangle'.

13. **convertibile:** a logical term first found in Apuleius. For the dative cf. Boethius' use with the verb: *non est dubium quin illa quae sunt aequalia sibi possint converti* (*In Isag.Porph.* ed.II,i,27).

19. **utrumque:** i.e. the fire and the hot body.

30. **praedicatum univocum:** on the question of univocity or otherwise of the predicate *ens,* see the second extract from Ockham. The point here is that Aquinas' argument would not apply to equivocal predicates, since one word with two significations could be applied *secundum quod est* to two different things: e.g. 'pig' can be properly used of an animal and a lump of smelted metal. Aquinas argues that *ens* is predicated either properly or analogically, but not equivocally.

52. **factivus:** the adverb *factive* is found in the glossaries, and the adjective was used in older translations of Aristotle for the Greek *poietikos.*

54. **actualitate:** another schoolman's term I have not traced earlier than 13th c. - it was probably not available to Abelard. The adjective *actualis* was used in a different sense, as equivalent to the Greek *praktikos* - that is with the meaning from the noun *actus* - as early as Macrobius, but as 'actual' or 'in act' it is later (Latham gives it as 8th-c.).

55. **virtualiter:** The Dominicans' English translation has 'virtually', but in view of the colloquial usage of that word it might be better to use 'formally' here, though that is not philosophically strictly accurate. It is another term of the age: cf. Scotus, *Ordinatio,* Prol.10: *sed naturaliter intelligimus prima principia, in quibus virtualiter includuntur omnes conclusiones; ergo naturaliter possumus scire omnes conclusiones scibiles;* and Ockham, *In Sent.* III,9,9,S: *quia sicut sapientia creaturae continetur virtualiter in Deo,* and

interestingly Abelard, *Dialectica, divisio virtualis totius = divisio totius secundum formam.*

57. **natum esse:** 'of a nature to be'; cf. Ovid, *Met.* 15, 120: *quid meruere boves, animal..natum tolerare labores?* This last part of the paragraph says that everything either is or is not from another; nothing can be both. If it is from another it exists contingently; if it is not from another it exists necessarily; but only God exists necessarily, therefore etc.

3. Aquinas: Science and Scripture:the rainbow
Quaestiones Quodlibetales, III q.14, a.1, ed. R. Spiazzi,
Turin 1956.

QUAESTIO XIV
Et circa hoc quaesita sunt duo.
3 Primo de arcu nubium qui dicitur iris, utrum sit signum diluvii non futuri. Secundo utrum possit demonstrative probari quod mundus non sit aeternus.
6 Circa primum sic proceditur: VIDETUR QUOD
ARCUS NUBIUM NON SIT SIGNUM DILUVII
NON FUTURI.
9 Illud enim quod fit ex necessitate naturae, non videtur
esse institutum ad aliud significandum. Sed arcus
nubium provenit ex necessitate naturae propter oppos-
12 itionem solis ad nubem roridam. Ergo non videtur
esse significativum diluvii non futuri.
    Praeterea, huiusmodi apparitiones aeris, sicut iris et
15 halo, id est circulus continens solem et lunam, et alia
huiusmodi, causantur praecipue ex vaporibus humidis
in aere existentibus, ex quibus sequuntur pluviae,
18 quae diluvium faciunt. Ergo apparitio iridis magis est
signum diluvii futuri.
    Praeterea, si est signum diluvii non futuri; aut est
21 signum diluvii nunquam futuri; aut est signum diluvii
non futuri usque ad aliquod tempus. Si autem est signum diluvii nunquam futuri, non oportuisset quod ap-
24 paruisset nisi semel; si autem diluvii non futuri usque
ad aliquod tempus, oporteret tempus esse determinatum; quod quidem determinari non potest nec aucto-
27 ritate Scripturae, nec ratione humana. Ergo frustra
huiusmodi signum datur.
    SED CONTRA, est quod dicitur Genes. IX,13:
30 *Arcum meum ponam in nubibus, et erit signum foe-*
deris inter me et inter terram ; et postea subditur (15):
Et non erunt ultra aquae diluvii ad delendum univer-
33 *sam carnem* .
    RESPONDEO. Dicendum, quod in his quae in
veteri testamento dicuntur, primo quidem observanda
36 est veritas litteralis. Sed quia vetus testamentum est

figura novi, plerumque in veteri testamento sic aliqua proponuntur, ut ipse modus loquendi aliquid figurate
39 designet.

Dicendum est ergo quod quia causae rerum multos latent, effectus autem sunt manifestiores, proponuntur
42 effectus in designationem causarum.

Est autem considerandum, quod pluviarum causa efficiens quidem est sol, materialis vero vapor humi-
45 dus elevatus ex terra et aquis per virtutem solis.

Haec autem duo in triplici dispositione se possunt habere.
48 Quandoque enim calor solis omnino supervincit vapores et exsiccat eos: et tunc pluviae sequi non possunt; unde in Aegypto et in terris multum calidis
51 non sunt pluviae; in aestate etiam propter propinquita- tem solis sunt pluviae rariores, in hieme vero frequen- tiores.
54 Quandoque vero e contrario virtus solis ad hoc usque valet quod vapores multiplicat, sed tamen non potest eos desiccare: et tunc superabundant pluviae, et
57 est ratio diluvii aquarum.

Quandoque vero medio modo se habet: ut scilicet virtus solis non solum operetur ad elevationem vapo-
60 rum, sed etiam habet victoriam super eos, ut non tan- tum multiplicentur quod diluvium inducere possint, neque etiam vapores omnino desiccentur ut pluvia non
63 sequatur; et ex hac media dispositione, vel compara- tione solis ad vapores causatur iris, quae non apparet vaporibus omnino desiccatis, neque etiam eis omnino
66 in aere superabundantibus. Et ideo iris est signum diluvii non futuri, in quantum procedit ex tali causa quae repugnat diluvio.
69 Ideo autem Scriptura tali modo loquendi utitur, quia per iridem significatur Christus, per quem protegimur a spirituali diluvio.
72 AD PRIMUM ergo dicendum, quod iris procedit naturaliter ex talibus causis quae repugnant diluvio; et ideo convenienter iris dicitur esse signum diluvii non
75 futuri.

AD SECUNDUM dicendum, quod iris potest sig-

nificare pluvias, sed non superabundanter usque ad
78 hoc quod faciant diluvium.

AD TERTIUM dicendum, quod iris semel apparens
significat quod tamdiu non erit diluvium, quamdiu sol
81 et vapores in eadem dispositione consistunt: et ideo
non est superfluum quod frequenter apparet.

Notes

3. **arcu nubium:** cf. Genesis 9,13, quoted below. The
usual medieval term is *arcus celestis,* or simply *iris*
(from Seneca on).

13. **significativum:** *signum* is used by Livy, Tacitus
and Seneca with nouns and participles (usually past)
in the genitive, in the sense of 'a sign that', equivalent
to a noun clause. The adjective is similarly used in the
Digest.

14. **apparitiones:** in the sense of 'appearances' only in
Christian writers, from Tertullian on.

15. **halo:** Seneca, *Q.N.* I,2,1: *hunc (circulum varii colo-
ris circa solem visum) Graeci halo vocant, nos dicere
coronam aptissime possumus.* The Greek is *halos,*
with the accusative as here, *halo* ; but in LL it became
halo, halonis (as some Romance languages testify)
some time before the 13th c. A halo is a kind of 'rainbow' round the sun or the moon caused by refraction
of the light through ice crystals in the upper atmo-
sphere.

18. **magis:** used for *potius* ='rather'; obviously common
since it led to the Fr. and It. *mais, ma* 'but'. It is used
by literary writers from Augustine on. Spiazzi's text
has here *signum diluvii non futuri,* which must be
wrong.

31. *inter me et inter terram:* *inter* is occasionally
used so repeated in CL. See L.& S. s.v. II B 1 fin.
Here the Latin versions follow the Hebrew.

32. *ad delendum universam carnem:* so older and
more recent editions of the Vulgate, though some
amend to *delendam.* The gerund with a direct object in
the accusative (of which we have had a number of

examples) is common in all periods except the short 'golden age' when it was presumably felt to be vulgar.

43. causa efficiens..materialis vero: two of Aristotle's four 'causes'. Cf. note on line 21 of the first Bonaventure extract.

48. supervincit: this, with *superabundare, superabundanter* (lines 56 and 77), are words from the oldest stratum of Christian Latin, from Tertullian on.

63. comparatione: a use of the word to mean 'proportion', 'correlation' (here almost 'equalisation'), probably from Albertus Magnus.

74. convenienter: 'consistently'; see L.& S. s.v. *convenio* under *conveniens* A, and cf. *inconventia* , 'inconsistency' in line 27 of the first Aquinas extract.

9. JOHN DUNS SCOTUS

Although down to the 10th and probably 11th century *Scotus* (or *Scottus*) denoted an Irishman, it later meant Scot in the modern sense. John Duns Scotus, the *Doctor subtilis,* whose surname, thanks to the Age of Enlightenment's distaste for his fine and sometimes involved reasoning, has in the form of 'dunce' become a sign for stupidity and ignorance, was a Scot. He was probably born on the south bank of the Tweed near Maxton in Roxburghshire in or about 1266. He was educated by the Franciscans at Dumfries, where he entered the order in 1281; ten years later he was ordained priest at Lincoln, and proceeded to study in Paris. After four years he came back to Oxford (or possibly first to Cambridge), there to compose his first commentary on the Sentences. In 1302-03 he was teaching in Paris; and in the latter year, having refused to support the king against the Pope in Avignon, he was forced to leave France, and the next thing we know is that he was in Cologne early in 1307. There he died on 8 November 1308.

His works fall into three main categories. First and foremost are the commentaries on the Sentences. Those from his Oxford years, collectively known as the *Opus Oxoniense,* were published about 1300-02. They comprise not one work, but several, of different kinds. The final form the commentary takes is the *Ordinatio,* the official commentary, as it were, edited and published by Scotus himself. An earlier form is the *Reportatio,* probably derived from pupils' writings, their notes on his teaching. What is probably the *Reportatio* of his Oxford lectures is usually known as the *Lectura* : the *Reportatio Magna* is the *Reportata Parisiensia,* belonging to his time in Paris, in various different versions. To these commentaries are attached the *Additiones,* Scotus' own additions and emendations added at various times. The second group of writings is a number of isolated disputations, *quaestiones quodlibetales,* and reports (*collationes*) of a number of *quaestiones* possibly privately discussed in the Franciscan houses in Paris and Oxford; 19 are from Paris and 27 from Oxford. Thirdly, there are the minor works: a few small treatises such as the *De Primo Principio* ; the commentary on Aristotle (*quaestiones* on the *Metaphysics* and probably the *De Anima*); possibly some logical writings; and a number of doubtful or clearly spurious works going under the name of Scotus.

The *Ordinatio* starts with the 13th-c. question:'Is philosophy sufficient for man?'. It is a question which did not arise in earlier times, and could only be asked after the schoolmen had read Aristotle. There they found themselves faced for the first time with a complete ancient system of philosophy, wholly worked out before and without revelation. Was it enough, was it all a man needed to live rightly? Scotus' formulation of the question is *Quaeritur utrum homini pro statu isto sit necessarium aliquam doctrinam specialem supernaturaliter inspirari, ad quam videlicet non posset attingere lumine naturali intellectus.* The phrase *pro statu isto* is important: we are concerned with man <u>as he is</u>, in his fallen state (if redeemed), not as he might have been when first created. Scotus distinguishes (in §5 of Part 1 of the Prologue) the attitudes of philosophers and theologians: *In ista quaestione videtur controversia inter philosophos et theologos. Et tenent philosophi perfectionem naturae, et negant perfectionem supernaturalem; theologi vero cognoscunt defectum naturae et necessitatem gratiae et perfectionem supernaturalem.* The arguments for and against the self-sufficiency of human reason include an addition by Scotus to his first draft (§12): *Nota, nullum supernaturale potest ratione naturali ostendi inesse viatori, nec necessario requiri ad perfectionem eius; nec etiam habens potest cognoscere illud sibi inesse. Igitur impossibile est hic contra Aristotelem uti ratione naturali: si arguatur ex creditis, non est ratio contra philosophum, quia praemissam creditam non concedet. Unde istae rationes hic factae contra ipsum alteram praemissam habent creditam vel probatam ex credito; ideo non sunt nisi persuasiones theologicae, ex creditis ad creditum.* There is in Scotus a blend of the 13th-c. distinction with an Augustinian sense of the necessity for the grace of understanding and the insufficiency of philosophy, rational thought, on its own. Our extract illustrates some of Scotus' arguments, and in particular it shows how the great authority of Augustine had to be respected and preserved even when one was disagreeing, if only by rephrasing what Augustine 'must have meant' - a device well known in politics. There is only one, long extract because for Scotus more than the others one needs to see the mind at work over a stretch to appreciate its subtlety and depth: not for nothing was he called the *Doctor subtilis.* But he repays effort: his was one of the greatest minds of the Middle Ages.

BIBLIOGRAPHY

There is no good single volume introduction to Duns Scotus; nor indeed can there be until the Vatican edition has been completed and assimilated. Perhaps the best short surveys are in the second volume of F.C. Copleston's *A History of Philosophy*, London 1950 and the very useful volume of selections in Nelson's Philosophical Texts, *Duns Scotus: Philosophical Writings*, by A.Wolter, Edinburgh 1962.

Scotus: Problems of Knowledge and Authority
Ordinatio I Dist.3 Pars 1 Q.4. ed. C. Balic, Vatican 1954

Ultimo - quantum ad materiam istam cognoscibilitatis
- quaero an aliqua veritas certa et sincera possit natu-
3   raliter cognosci ab intellectu viatoris, absque lucis increatae speciali illustratione.
Arguo quod non: IX *De Trinitate* cap.6 vel 15: 'Intu-
6   eamur inviolabilem veritatem, ex qua definiamus qualis esse mens hominis sempiternis rationibus debeat'.
Et ibidem, cap.15: 'Aliis supra nos regulis manenti-
9   bus vel approbare vel improbare convincimur, quando
aliquid, recte vel non recte, probamus vel improba-
mus'. Et ibidem, cap.17: 'Artem ineffabiliter pul-
12   chram, super aciem mentis, simplici intelligentia capientes'. Et eodem, cap.8 vel 18: 'In illa veritate, ex qua
temporalia sunt facta omnia, formam conspicimus, at-
15   que inde conceptam veracem notitiam tamquam
"verbum" apud nos habemus'.
Item, libro XII cap.2:'Sublimioris rationis est iudicare
18   de istis corporalibus secundum rationes sempiternas'.
Item, in eodem XII cap.14 vel 32: 'Non solum rerum
sensibilium, in locis positarum, stant incommutabiles
21   rationes' etc. Et quod intelligat ibi de rationibus aeternis vere in Deo, probatur per hoc quod ibidem dicit
quod 'paucorum est ad illas pervenire'; si autem intel-
24   ligeret de primis principiis, non est paucorum pervenire ad illa, sed multorum, quia omnibus sunt com-
munia et nota.
27   Item, libro XIV cap.15 vel 34, loquens de iniusto, qui
'multa recte laudat et vituperat in moribus hominum',
ait: 'Quibus regulis iudicat?' etc.; et in fine ait: 'Ubi
30   sunt illae regulae scriptae, nisi in libro illo lucis?' -
Liber ille lucis est intellectus divinus; igitur vult ut in
illa luce iniustus videt quae sunt iuste agenda, et quod
33   in aliquo impresso vel per aliquod impressum ab illo,
videtur, ut ibidem dicit: 'unde omnis lex iusta in cor
hominis non migrando sed tamquam imprimendo
36   transfertur, sicut imago ex anulo et in ceram transit et
ceram non relinquit'. Igitur in illa luce videmus, a qua

39 imprimitur in cor hominis iustitia. Illa autem est lux increata.

42 Item, XII *Confessionum* : 'Si ambo videmus "verum" nec tu in me nec ego in te, sed ambo in ea quae supra mentem est, incommutabili veritate'. Multae autem sunt auctoritates Augustini, in multis locis, ad probandum hanc conclusionem.

45 Ad oppositum: Rom. 1: *Invisibilia Dei a creatura mundi per ea quae facta sunt intellecta conspiciuntur.* Istae 'rationes aeternae' sunt *invisibilia Dei*, ergo cog-

48 noscuntur ex creaturis; igitur ante visionem istarum habetur certa cognitio creaturarum.

Et ex isto apparet qualiter non est necessaria specialis

51 illustratio ad videndum in regulis aeternis, quia Augustinus non ponit in eis videri nisi 'vera' quae sunt necessaria ex vi terminorum. Et in talibus est maxima

54 naturalitas - tam causae remotae quam proximae - respectu affectus, puta tam intellectus divini ad obiecta moventia quam illorum obiectiorum ad veritatem com-

57 plexionis de eis. Et etiam, licet non tanta sit naturalitas ad perceptionem illius veritatis quod 'oppositum contradictionem includat', tamen naturalitas est a parte

60 causae proximae, coassistente sibi causa remota, quia termini apprehensi et compositi, sunt nati naturaliter causare evidentiam conformitatis compositionis ad ter-

63 minos. Et si ponatur quod Deus coagat terminis ad hunc effectum influentia generali, non tamen necessitate naturali: sed, sive sit influentia generalis sive -

66 quod plus est - necessitas naturalis influendi terminis ad hunc effectum, patet quod non requiritur illustratio specialis.

69 Assumptum de intentione Augustini patet per ipsum, IV *De Trinitate* cap.35(loquitur de philosophis): 'Nonnulli eorum potuerunt aciem mentis ultra omnem crea-

72 turam levare, et lucem incommutabilis veritatis quantulacumque ex parte attingere, qui christianos multos, ex sola fide viventes, nondum posse derident'. Ergo

75   vult quod christiani credita non vident in regulis aeternis, sed philosophi vident in illis necessaria multa.
Idem etiam IX *De Trinitate* cap.6: 'Non qualis unius-
78   cuiusque hominis mens' etc.; quasi diceret: contingentia non videntur ibi, sed necessaria.
Et in eodem IV cap.36 arguit contra istos philosophos
81   'Numquid quia verissime disputant "aeternis rationibus omnia temporalia fieri", propterea potuerunt in
ipsis rationibus aspicere quot sunt animalium genera,
84   quot semina singulorum in exordiis?' etc. 'Nonne ista
omnia, non per illam incommutabilem scientiam sed
per locorum ac temporum historiam quaesierunt, et ab
87   aliis experta atque conscripta crediderunt?' Ergo intelligit quod per regulas aeternas non cognoscuntur illa
contingentia quae tantum per sensus cognoscuntur vel
90   per historias creduntur, - et tamen specialis illustratio
magis requiritur in credendis quam in cognitis neces-
sariis: immo ibi maxime removetur illustratio specialis
93   et sufficit sola generalis.
Contra: quid igitur dicit Augustinus XII *De Trinitate*
cap.14, quod 'paucorum est mentis acie pervenire ad
96   rationes intelligibiles'?- et 83*Quaestionum* quaestione
46, 'non nisi purae animae ad illas pertingunt'?
Respondeo: ista 'puritas' non debet intelligi a vitiis -
99   quia XIV *De Trinitate* cap.15 vult quod iniustus videt
in regulis aeternis quid iustum faciendum sit, et IV
libro capitulo praeallegato vult quod philosophi vident
102 veritatem in regulis aeternis sine fide, et quaestione
eadem vult quod nullus potest esse sapiens sine cognitione idearum (eo modo quo Platonem concederent,
105 forsan, sapientem esse) - sed ista 'puritas' debet intelligi elevando intellectum ad considerandum veritates
ut relucent in se, non tantum ut relucent in phantas-
108 mate.
Ubi considerandum est quod res sensibilis, extra,
causat phantasma 'confusum' et 'unum' per accidens,
111 in virtute phantastica, repraesentans scilicet rem secundum quantitatem, secundum figuram et colorem et
alia accidentia sensibilia. Et sicut phantasma repraes-
114 sentat tantum confuse et per accidens, ita multi perci-

piunt tantum 'ens per accidens'. Veritates autem primae sunt praecise tales ex propria ratione terminorum
117 in quantum illi termini abstrahuntur ab omnibus per
accidens coniunctis cum eis. Non enim haec propositio 'omne totum est maius sua parte' primo vera est
120 ut 'totum' est in lapide vel ligno, sed ut 'totum' abs-
trahitur ab omnibus quibus coniungitur per accidens.
Et ideo intellectus qui numquam intelligit totalitatem
123 nisi in 'conceptu per accidens', puta in totalitate lapi-
dis vel ligni, numquam intelligit sinceram veritatem
huius principii, quia numquam intelligit praecisam
126 rationem termini per quam est veritas.
'Paucorum' ergo est pertingere ad rationes aeternas,
quia paucorum est habere 'intellectiones per se', et
129 multorum est habere 'conceptus' tales 'per accidens'.
Sed isti 'pauci' non dicuntur distingui ab aliis propter
specialem illustrationem, sed vel propter meliora natu-
132 ralia (quia habent intellectum magis abstrahentem et
magis perspicacem)vel propter maiorem inquisitionem
per quam aeque ingeniosus pervenit ad cognoscen-
135 dum illas quiditates quas alius, non inquirens, non
cognoscit. Et isto modo intelligitur illud Augustini IX
De Trinitate cap.6, de vidente in monte et vidente in-
138 ferius aerem nebulosum et superius lucem sinceram.
Qui enim tantum intelligit semper 'conceptus per accidens' eo modo quo phantasma repraesentat obiecta
141 talia quasi 'entia per accidens' - ipse est quasi in valle,
circumdatus aere nebuloso. Sed qui separat quiditates
intelligendo praecise eas conceptu per se - quae tamen
144 relucent in phantasmate cum multis aliis accidentibus
adiunctis - ipse habet phantasma inferius quasi aerem
nebulosum: et ipse est in 'monte' in quantum cognos-
147 cit illam veritatem, et videt 'verum supra' ut illam veritatem superiorem in virtute intellectus increati, quae
est lux aeterna.
150 Ultimo modo, potest concedi quod cognoscuntur veritates sincerae in luce aeterna sicut in obiecto remoto
cognito, quia lux increata est primum principium
153 entium speculabilium et ultimus finis rerum practi-
carum: et ideo ab ipso sumuntur principia prima, tam

speculabilia quam practica, - et ideo cognitio omnium,
156 tam speculabilium quam practicabilium, per principia
sumpta a luce aeterna ut cognita, est perfectior et
purior cognitione sumpta per principia in genere pro-
159 prio. Et hoc modo cognitio omnium pertinet ad theo-
logum, sicut dictum est in quaestione illa de subiecto
theologiae, et est eminentior alia quacumque. Hoc
162 modo sincera veritas cognosci dicitur, quia per illud
cognoscitur quod est tantum veritas, non habens aliquid permixtum non-veritatis, quia per primum ens, a
165 quo cognito sumuntur principia sic cognoscendi; aliud
autem quodcumque, a quo sumuntur principia cognoscendi in genere, est 'verum' defectivum. Hoc
168 modo solus Deus cognoscit omnia tantum sincere,
quia, ut dictum est in quaestione de subiecto theologiae, solus ipse novit omnia praecise per essentiam
171 suam; omnis alius intellectus moveri potest ab obiecto
alio ad cognoscendum veritatem aliquam virtute eius.
Cognoscere enim triangulum 'habere tres' ut est quae-
174 dam participatio Dei et habens talem ordinem in universo quod quasi perfectius exprimit perfectionem
Dei, hoc est nobiliori modo cognoscere triangulum
177 'habere tres' quam per rationem trianguli; et ita cognoscere quod 'temperate vivendum est' propter beatitu-
dinem ultimam consequendam, quae est attingendo
180 essentiam Dei in se, perfectius est cognoscere istud
cognoscibile practicum quam per principium aliquod
in genere moris, puta per hoc quod 'honeste viven-
183 dum est'.
Et isto modo loquitur Augustinus de luce increata ut
cognita, XV *De Trinitate* cap.27 vel 82, ubi se ipsum
186 alloquens ait: 'Multa vera vidisti, et ea, quae discrevisti ab ista luce, qua tibi lucente vidisti. Attolle
oculos ad ipsam lucem et eos in eam fige, si potes: sic
189 enim videbis quomodo distat nativitas Verbi Dei a
processione Doni Dei'; et paulo post: 'Haec et alia
oculis tuis interioribus lux ista monstravit. Quae est
192 ergo causa cur acie fixa ipsam videre non poteris, nisi
utique infirmitas?' etc.
Ex dictis patet ad omnes auctoritates Augustini 'ad

195 oppositum', et secundum aliquem dictorum modorum
videndi 'in' exponi possunt auctoritates Augustini
quae occurrunt de ista materia.

Notes

Wolter's translation (pp.97ff.) should be treated with some
care: it is not always accurate. The second references to the
De Trinitate of Augustine are to the Corpus Christianorum
ed. by W.J. Mountain (CC 50, 50A); 'cf.' before a
reference means that Scotus has adapted or paraphrased to
some extent.

1. **istam:** in popular and LL *iste* is very often used for
    hic, and frequently, like *ipse, ille,* simply as a definite
    article; it is not much more here. See the interesting
    note in P.B. Corbett, *The Latin of the Regula
    Magistri*, Louvain 1958, pp.135ff.
    cognoscibilitatis: *cognoscibilis* is in Boethius,
    cognoscibiliter in the Vulgate; *cognoscibilitas* may be
    13th-c., but it looks older. *Materia cognoscibilitatis*
    means 'what can be known'.
3. **viatoris:** i.e. man *pro statu isto;* a use of the word
    perhaps derived from its use on tombstones (*siste,
    viator*) and obviously referring there as here to a man
    as a traveller through this world on his way to his
    proper country, Heaven.
4. **illustratione:**'enlightenment'; in the literal, physical
    sense in Chalcidius, and metaphorically from Gregory
    the Great on.
    Cf. *De Trin.* IX, vi, 9, 5-18.
8. Cf. *ib.* 10, 22-25.
11. *ib.* 11, 77-79.
12. **capientes:** it is easier to translate 'we grasp'.
13. **eodem:** 'in the same place'; L.&. S. s.v. I. *De Trin.*
    IX, vii, 12, 1-6.
    ex qua: note the Platonic Ideas in the Logos, almost
    a medieval commonplace; and cf. line 81.
17. Cf. *De Trin.* XII, ii, 2, 16-17.
19. Cf. *ib.* xiv, 23, 54-59.

21. **et quod:** 'and that'.
   intelligat: 'he is thinking' **de** 'about'.
27. Cf. *De Trin.* XIV, xv, 21, 38-40; 49-53.
31. **igitur:** does not modify *vult,* but the sentence: 'and
   so it follows that', 'therefore we can say that';
   vult ut: 'he means that' (see L.&. S. s.v. *volo* I B
   3)*vult quod* in line 75 and elsewhere means the same,
   like the *vult ut..et quod* here.
33. **ab illo:** with this punctuation *ab illo* is taken with
   impressum (and *impresso*), and must refer to the
   intellectus divinus (line 31); and *videtur* must be
   passive: 'it is seen' (i.e. *quae sunt iuste agenda*).
37. **ceram:** editor's note: *loco 'ceram' in libro Augustini
   reperies 'anulum'* (which is obviously right).
40. *Conf.* XII, 25, 35 (PL 32, 840: CSEL 33, 336, 2-6).
43. **auctoritates:** here must mean 'passages'; the use is
   derived from the citing of *auctoritates* in the schools
   and their collection in florilegia for the use of masters
   and students. Cf. L.& S. s.v. II G 2.
45. *a creatura mundi:* Rom. 1, 20. *Creatura* has in
   Latin all the three senses: (a) creation, the act of
   creating; (b) the creation, the whole that was made;
   (c) a creature, the thing made, as in line 48.
50. What follows is the last part of the 'body' of the
   Quaestio, after which come the replies to arguments
   used to oppose the thesis. The complex arguments in
   between are on pp. 99-126 of Wolter.
   qualiter: 'how', almost, as often in English, 'why'.
54. **naturalitas:** here must be equivalent to *necessitas* ;
   what is 'by nature' is also in a sense necessary (which
   is why Pliny can use *mors naturalis* for Cicero's
   mors necessaria); and what is 'necessary' in nature is
   also 'natural'. Cf. the use of *naturaliter* in line 61.
55. **affectus:** genitive. In Latin *effectus* is active,
   affectus passive, = 'effect'. The *causa remota* in this
   passage is the *intellectus divinus,* with respect to the
   objects which move our intellects; the *causa proxima*
   is the objects themselves with respect to the truth of a
   proposition (*complexio*) about them.
56. **complexionis:** used by Cicero and others of the

conclusion of a syllogism, and reasonably extended to mean any proposition, something 'twining together' terms. So also *compositio* (line 62) a 'putting together' of terms.

58. quod: 'that'.

oppositum: nominative noun, 'its opposite'; from the Schools' definition of a necessary proposition as one the opposite of which was self-contradictory.

60. coassistente: the *sibi* must refer to *causae proximae; coassistente* means more than simply 'co-existing' - 'assisting' rather. Cf. L.&. S. s.v. *assisto* II B a. So used from 12th c.

63. coagat: 'works with' the terms; so Albertus Magnus and others.

66. influendi: the meaning 'influence' was probably derived from its astrological use, since heavenly influences were thought of as actually 'flowing from' the planets: *terminis* is presumably dative.

69. assumptum: 'what is assumed'; cf. *De Trin.* IV, xix, 20, 11-15. The philosophers are clearly 'the Platonists' i.e. Neoplatonists.

73. qui: the connecting relative 'and they'.

77. *De Trin.* IX, vi, 9, 17; 15-18 read: *intuemur inviolabilem veritatem ex qua perfecte quantum possumus definiamus non qualis sit uniuscuiusque hominis mens, sed qualis esse sempiternis rationibus debeat.*

80. Cf. *ib.* IV, xvi, 21, 6-10, 13-16.

86. historiam: 'an account' - used in the same sense as in Pliny's title, *Naturalis Historia*.

92. immo ibi: 'indeed there (i.e. with necessary truths) there is least need for special illumination'.

94. Cf. *De Trin.* XII, xiv, 23, 58-59. *Dicit* = 'means', not 'says'(L.&. S. s.v. II).

96. *De Div.Quaest.* lxxxiii, Q.46,2; PL 40, 30.

98. a vitiis: that is, as *puritas a vitiis;* an extension of the *a* + abl. from the Silver Latin use with *purus*.

99. Cf. *De Trin.* XIV, xv, 21, 37-42.

100 *De Trin.* IV, xv, 20, 11-14.

101 Praeallegato = 'aforementioned'; CL *allegare* is used to mean 'to mention' in Silver Latin.

106 elevando: it might be possible to explain the ablative by the ellipse of some word of achievement: 'this purity should be understood as (being achieved) by raising'; but it is much more likely simply 'absolute', almost indeclinable: 'be understood as raising'.

107 phantasmate: any image or appearance; L.& S. is misleading. Here it is used by a philosopher with Plato in mind, and it means appearance as opposed to the reality of Ideas. The *virtus phantastica* in line 111 is the 'faculty of the imagination' where 'imagination' means the making of images in the mind - the image in the mind of the horse or table or whatever, which is seen, and which is itself for Plato the image of the Idea.

116 tales: i.e. *primae; praecise* must here have its modern sense, 'precisely', derived from its meaning 'briefly', 'concisely'.

122 totalitatem: common in 12th and 13th-c. schools, but surely much older.

128 intellectiones: used in this sense (almost equivalent to *rationes*) by Tertullian and by Priscian, and possibly a century or so older.

136 *De Trin.* IX, vi, 11.

142 sed qui..: 'but he who separates out the essences, understanding them precisely by conceiving them in themselves, although they..'; *conceptu* is more verbal than nominal, as often, and *eas* is taken both with *intelligendo* and with *conceptu.*

153 speculabilium: used here in the literal sense of 'seeable' in Statius, *Theb.* XII, 624; here opposed to *practica* it must mean 'things thought' as against 'things done'.

156 practicabilium: possibly Scotus' own word, but the verb *practicare* from CL *practicus* is centuries older.

158 principia in genere proprio: 'principles from their own kind of things'.

160 quaestione illa: Scotus, *Ord.* prol. 206(vol.I, 138-39). From *sicut dictum est* to *aliquam virtute eius* (line 172) is an addition by Scotus to his original version.

162 per illud..quod est: 'through this..that it is..';
quia (line 164) sc. *cognoscitur:* 'because it is known
through the first being, from which once it is known'.

164 non-veritatis: this may look like a very modern use
of *non,* but even Cicero can write *non corpus* (which
perhaps should be hyphenated) 'that which is not
body'.

168 tantum sincere: with no mixture, that is, of
'objects'.

169 quaestione: Scotus, *Ord*.prol. 200-201 (vol.I,135-
36).

172 virtute eius: sc. *Dei.*

173 habere tres: sc. *angulos duobus rectis aequales;*
ut est: 'as it is', 'because it is';

174 talem..quod: 'such..that..'
ordinem in universo:'a rank in the whole' or 'in
the universe' - the triangle is the first plane figure and
obviously symbolises the First Being, the Trinity.

179 attingendo: another 'absolute' gerund:'the attain-
ment of'.

184 Cf. *De Trin.* XV, 27, 50, 82-85, and PL 42, 1097.
The Augustine texts have not: *multa vera vidisti, et ea,
quae discrevisti* but *multa vera vidisti eaque discrevisti.* The *ea quae* goes back at least to the 10th-c.
MS **P.**

186 The punctuation is that of the Vatican ed. Wolter
prints Scotus' text, punctuates differently and translates the PL text of the *De Trinitate.* As it stands, the
meaning must be: 'You have seen many truths, and
those which you distinguished from that light (which
you discerned by that light?) you have seen by its
shining on you'.

190 et paulo post: *De Trin.* XV, 27, 50, 112-15.

194 patet ad: presumably understand a subject *respon-
sum.*

10. WILLIAM OF OCKHAM

Ockham's life is mostly to be guessed at from scattered evidence, but a plausible picture can be built up, and there are some firm facts and dates. He may have been born at Ockham in Surrey, and since he was ordained subdeacon in 1306 he was presumably born in the early or mid-1280s. He certainly studied and taught at Oxford from about 1309, including lecturing on the Sentences from 1317 or thereabouts. He left Oxford for the Franciscan house in London about 1321; though he qualified as a Master in Theology he never 'incepted' - that is, began teaching as a *Magister Regens* at Oxford, so remaining an *Inceptor:* hence his common title, *Venerabilis Inceptor*. He most likely left Oxford because of the hostility of of the Thomist ('an over-zealous Thomist' Boehner says) Chancellor, John Lutterell. The same Lutterell, now deposed as Chancellor, went in 1323 to the papal court at Avignon to accuse Ockham of heresy, and Ockham was summoned to Avignon in the following year. Four years later (he probably lived with the Franciscans at Avignon, still uncondemned and arguing) he fled with Michael of Cesena, the General of the Order, to Munich, to the Emperor Ludwig of Bavaria. Ockham had become involved in the quarrel between some of the Franciscans under Michael and the rest, with the Pope, over the question of their angelical and apostolic poverty; a quarrel Ludwig was quite willing to join in, having just been crowned Emperor in Rome by an anti-pope of his own appointing. Michael died in 1342, and in 1347 so did Ludwig of Bavaria. Ockham, isolated and hopeless, submitted to the Pope - without, however, acknowledging any errors in his teaching beyond those concerning relations between Pope and Emperor. Soon after this he himself died, still in Munich, possibly of the Black Death.

Ockham was the greatest of the medieval logicians, and carried much further that divorce of formal logic from metaphysics which had been begun by Abelard 200 years earlier. Ockham's conception of logic, says Leff (p.xviii) 'was central to his outlook, not through reducing all problems to questions of logic or in the formal sense of approaching them logically - all scholastics did that - but as the means of ordering all knowledge and of ascertaining the different degrees of certainty which men can have'. In Ockham that withdrawal from the great confidence in Reason's ability to comprehend Reality characteristic of the 13th century was taken so far that Theology became more and more divorced from and superior to logical enquiry. Boehner (p.xviii) quotes his *De Corpore Christi:* 'I consider it to be dangerous and temerarious to force anyone to fetter his mind and to believe something which his reason dictates to him to be false, unless it can be drawn from holy scripture or from a determination of the Roman church or from the words of approved doctors'. Ockham's physics and metaphysics were firmly based on the reality of and only of the individual created thing (apart from the realm of the eternal). As Leff says (p.xx), his thought 'is founded upon the discrepancy between the conceptual and the ontological, expressed in the contrast between the individual nature of all being and the universal nature of our concepts and terms constituting proper knowledge of it'.

Ockham's famous 'razor', it may be mentioned, (a principle of economy which was around in the schools before him) was expressed in various ways by him, the briefest and commonest being: *frustra fit per plura quod fieri potest per pauciora.* It seems not to occur in the form so often alleged to be Ockham's: *entia non sunt multiplicanda praeter necessitatem.* The consequent removal of the 'concept', the universal, from his dialectic left the logician dealing only with terms and propositions, not ideas: 'man' is a universal term because it is predicable of pronouns demonstrating many things taken singly. It is so because in the act of knowing a man (a single individual man, which is all that can be directly known) the act of knowing is itself the 'universal' by which we recognise the individual as a man and use the predicate 'man' in saying of him:'This is a man'. Problems of the existence or non-existence of universals therefore do not arise. Knowledge of 'existence' is intuitive: and Ockham's intuition is that which enables us to judge that a thing exists, when it does, and that a thing does not exist, when it does not. Knowledge in the non-intuitive sense of *scientia* is for Ockham what it had been for Aristotle, derived syllogistically from certain, evident and necessary premises.

Of the transcendence and absoluteness of God and of his power Ockham is utterly certain: and that God is First Being is fully accepted. But since there is no such thing as Being, there are only beings, 'being' is an abstraction, an abstract cognition. So too, is 'firstness'; the two combined give us a concept applicable to God. The term 'being' must be used in the same sense, univocally, if there is to be any link between us and our knowledge and God. But he is in reality (as opposed to what we know and say of him) utterly different and transcendent. This is part of Ockham's 'Nominalism', his rejection of the reality of such things as universals and formal distinctions. Nominalism was a movement of thought in the 14th century, a development from, and reaction to, Scotus and Aquinas, and there were other important thinkers of the same kind, such as the great Franciscan Peter Aureoli (died c.1322), but Ockham is generally regarded as the most important founder of the movement.

BIBLIOGRAPHY

P. Boehner, *Ockham: Philosophical Writings,* Edinburgh 1957, has not only a good bibliography to that date, but an interesting introduction; as indeed has his edition of the *Tractatus de Praedestinatione,* New York 1945. G. Leff, *William of Ockham,* Manchester 1975, also has a very useful bibliography and introduction, though the very long exposition of Ockham's thought is perhaps less easy to read than Ockham's own writings.

1. Ockham: The foreknowledge of God
Tractatus de Praedestinatione, ed. P. Boehner

Sexta suppositio: quod indubitanter est tenendum
quod Deus certitudinaliter scit omnia futura contin-
3   gentia, ita quod certitudinaliter scit quae pars contradictionis erit vera et quae falsa, ita tamen quod omnes
tales propositiones 'Deus scit hanc partem contradic-
6   tionis esse veram' vel 'illam' sunt contingentes et non
necessariae, sicut prius dictum est. Sed difficile est
videre quomodo haec scit, cum una pars non plus de-
9   terminetur ad veritatem quam alia.
Et dicit Doctor Subtilis quod intellectus divinus, prout
quodammodo praecedit determinationem voluntatis
12   divinae, apprehendit illa complexa ut neutra, et voluntas determinat alteram partem esse veram pro aliquo
instanti, volens alteram partem esse veram pro eodem
15   instanti. Posita autem determinatione voluntatis, intellectus divinus videt determinationem voluntatis suae
quae est immutabilis: videt evidenter alteram partem
18   esse veram, illam scilicet quam voluntas sua vult esse
veram certitudinaliter.
Sed contra istam opinionem: quia non videtur salvare
21   certitudinem scientiae Dei respectu futurorum quae
simpliciter dependent a voluntate creata; quia quaero,
utrum illam determinationem voluntatis divinae neces-
24   sario sequatur determinatio voluntatis creatae aut non.
Si sic, igitur voluntas necessario ageret sicut ignis, et
ita tollitur meritum et demeritum. Si non, igitur ad sci-
27   endum determinate alteram partem contradictionis illorum requiritur determinatio voluntatis creatae, quia determinatio voluntatis increatae non sufficit, cum
30   voluntas creata possit in oppositum illius determinati-
onis. Igitur cum illa determinatio voluntatis non fuit
ab aeterno, non habuit Deus certam notitiam illorum.
33   Secundo sic: quando aliquid determinatur contingenter, ita quod adhuc possibile est non determinari, et
possibile est quod numquam fuisset determinatum,
36   propter talem determinationem non potest haberi certa
et infallibilis notitia; sed huiusmodi est determinatio

voluntatis divinae respectu futurorum contingentium
39 secundum eum et secundum veritatem; igitur propter
talem determinationem non potest haberi certa notitia a
Deo de futuris contingentibus.

42 Confirmatur: omnes tales sunt contingentes 'Deus ab
aeterno voluit hanc partem esse veram', 'Deus ab aeterno determinavit hoc' et huiusmodi - patet ex secun-
45 da suppositione - et possunt per consequens esse
verae et falsae; igitur propter talem determinationem
nulla habebitur certa notitia.

48 Ideo dico quod impossibile est clare exprimere
modum quo Deus scit futura contingentia. Tamen
tenendum est quod scit contingenter tantum. Et debet
51 istud teneri propter dicta Sanctorum, qui dicunt quod
Deus non aliter cognoscit fienda quam facta. Potest
tamen talis modus assignari, nam sicut ex eadem
54 notitia intuitiva aliquorum incomplexorum potest intellectus evidenter cognoscere propositiones contingentes contradictorias, puta quod a est, a non est, eodem
57 modo potest concedi quod essentia divina est notitia
intuitiva, quae est tam perfecta, tam clara quod ipsa
est notitia evidens omnium praeteritorum et futurorum
60 ita quod ipsa scit quae pars contradictionis erit vera et
quae pars falsa.

Si dicatur quod illud quod non est in se verum non
63 potest sciri ab aliquo; sed me sedere cras est huiusmodi; dico quod est vera, ita quod non falsa, tamen
est contingenter vera, quia potest esse falsa.

66 Contra: utraque pars istius 'ego sedebo cras, ego non
sedebo cras' indifferenter potest esse vera; igitur non
plus est una pars vera quam alia. Et sic neutra est
69 nunc vera vel utraque; non utraque, igitur neutra. Dico
quod una pars nunc determinate est vera, ita quod non
falsa, quia Deus vult unam partem esse veram et aliam
72 esse falsam. Tamen contingenter vult, et ideo potest
non velle illam partem, et partem aliam potest velle,
sicut pars alia potest evenire.

Notes

2. **certitudinaliter:** 13th-c. It occurs in William of
Moerbeke's translation of Proclus' commentary on
Plato's *Parmenides: solus autem intellectus certitudinaliter et perfecte tollere potest intelligibilem
speciem* (written 1280-85).

6. **contingentes:** that is contingent which is not
necessary, which might <u>not</u> be. As this technical term
of dialectic, *contingens* is found often in Boethius,
e.g. *De Interp.* ed. II v 12: *unde fit ut, cum possibile
atque contingens idem in significationibus sit, diver-
sum esse in enuntiationibus videatur.*

9. **alia:** despite the distinctions drawn by logicians
between *omnis* and *uterque, alius* and *alter,* they are
frequently ignored in practice.

10. **Doctor Subtilis:** Scotus, *Op.Oxon.* I, D.39, Q.
unica, and *Report.* I, D.38, Q.2. Cf. also Ockham,
Ordinatio, D.38, Q.1, printed by Boehner in App.1,
p.94 f., to his text of the *Tractatus.*

11. **determinationem:** the verb *determino* is found in
similar senses in Pliny, Tertullian and Minucius Felix,
and the noun in the last two; the phrase *determinate
verum* is found in Boethius.

12. **complexa:** i.e. propositions, as opposed to terms,
the *incomplexa* of line 54. Boehner's text has *complexa ut neutra sibi, et voluntas divina determinat* etc.
Brown omits *sibi*, which makes it easier, but also
divina after *voluntas.* He has a note on *veram* (14):
potius 'falsam' - which is surely correct.

21. **certitudinem:** the word seems to be 4th-c. It is used
by Augustine.

25. **Si sic:** cf. Ter. *Heaut.* IV,1,15 and L.&. S. s.v. *sic*
V, 5. Such a use, of course, is the origin of the
Romance languages *si* for 'yes'.

27. **illorum:** presumably refers to *futurorum* (21), and
should be taken with the following *determinatio.* The
word is missing from some of the best MSS.

30. **possit:** absolute = 'could act', common from 3rd c.

37. **infallibilis:** this cannot surely be a 13th-c. coinage:
it is found as an alternative reading for the correct *in-*

falsabilis in an early translation of an anonymous commentary on St. Matthew ascribed to Chrysostom, which at least demonstrates its availability to a scribe as a commoner word than *infalsabilis.*

39. secundum eum: i.e. Scotus.

44. patet ex secunda suppositione: Ockham in his second supposition states that Scotus proved (in his Oxford Commentary, the *Ordinatio,* I, D.39) that all such statements were contingent, as against Aquinas' teaching that both parts of the conditional sentence *Si Deus scivit aliquid, illud erit,* were necessary. For Scotus and most later Scholastics, past, present and future for us were also so in God's eternity; Aquinas held to the Boethian idea of God's eternal 'present'. Boehner says that so long as immutability and necessity are not confused, God's knowledge of future contingents can be contingent and immutable without being necessary.

50. contingenter: see note on line 6: the adverb is also Boethian. For the *dicta Sanctorum* cf. Ecclus. 42,19: *cognovit enim Deus omnem scientiam, et inspexit in signum aevi, adnuntians quae praeterierunt et quae superventura sunt, revelans vestigia occultorum;* and cf. Isaiah 41, 22 and 46, 10; Aug. *De Trin.* XV,7,13.

74. sicut: = *sic ut* (and should perhaps be printed separately) and hence precisely the equivalent of *ita quod;* cf. Cic.*Or.* 36,125: *omnis pars orationis esse debet laudabilis, sic ut verbum nullum excidat.*

2. Ockham: Being
Quodlibet V, Quaestio 14, ed. J.C. Wey, Guillelmi de Ockham Opera Philosophica et Theologica: Opera Theologica IX; Quodlibeta Septem, New York 1980

UTRUM 'ENS' PRAEDICETUR UNIVOCE DE OMNIBUS

3   Quod non: Quia aliqua sunt primo diversa quae in nullo conveniunt, puta Deus et creatura; igitur de illis non praedicetur univoce.

6   Contra: Nisi praedicetur univoce, aliter in primo principio esset aequivocatio.

    Ad istam quaestionem teneo duas conclusiones: prima

9   est quod huic nomini 'ens' correspondet unus conceptus communis praedicabilis de omnibus rebus.

    Quod probo, quia sit a homo, sit b animal, sit c

12   Sortes. Tunc arguo: sicut possunt formari tres propositiones tales vocales 'c est a', 'c est b', 'c est ens', ita possunt in mente similes tres propositiones formari,

15   quarum duae sint dubiae et tertia sit scita, quia possibile est quod aliquis dubitet utramque istarum 'c est a', 'c est b' et tamen quod sciat istam 'c est ens et ali-

18   quid'. Patet hoc manifeste de veniente a remotis, quod videns frequenter dubitat utrum sit homo vel animal vel asinus, et tamen evidenter scit quod est ens et ali-

21   quid.

    Hoc supposito, tunc arguo sic: duae istarum propositionum in mente sunt dubiae et tertia est scita, et istae

24   tres propositiones habent idem subiectum omnino, igitur habent distincta praedicata; aliter enim eadem propositio simul et semel esset dubia et certa uni et

27   eidem, quod est impossibile; igitur istae tres propositiones habent tria praedicata distincta. Similiter manifestum est quod praedicatum tertiae propositionis non

30   est minus commune nec convertibile cum aliquo aliorum praedicatorum; igitur est communius praedicatum quam aliquod istorum. Et hoc est propositum,

33   quod ille conceptus est alius ab inferioribus et communius eis, quia de pronomine demonstrante quodcumque ens potest ille conceptus vere praedicari, sicut

36 eadem vox potest vere de quolibet praedicari.
Secunda conclusio est quod hoc nomen 'ens' est ae-
quivocum, quia licet praedicetur univoce de omnibus
39 subicibilibus absolutis, et hoc sive supponant simpliciter vel personaliter, tamen non praedicatur de omnibus subicibilibus significative acceptis secundum
42 unum conceptum, sed huic nomini diversi conceptus
correspondent, sicut patebit alias.
Sed dico quod conceptus entis est univocus Deo et
45 omnibus aliis rebus. Quod patet, quia omnes con-
cedunt quod aliquam notitiam incomplexam habemus
de Deo. Tunc quaero: aut cognoscimus Deum in se et
48 sub propria ratione deitatis cognitione propria, simplici, absoluta et affirmativa; et hoc non est verum,
quia nec cognoscimus Deum sic cognitione intuitiva
51 nec abstractiva. De intuitiva patet. De abstractiva probatur, quia quaelibet talis cognitio abstractiva prae-
supponit intuitivam. Aut cognoscimus Deum, non in
54 se sicuti est, sed in aliquo conceptu; et tunc aut ille
conceptus erit simplex, et tunc erit communis, quia
non est proprius, et habetur propositum; aut erit con-
57 ceptus compositus, et tunc aliqua pars illius conceptus
compositi erit communis et simplex, quia ille conceptus compositus non componitur ex propriis concep-
60 tibus, igitur ex communibus. Et ita habetur propositum, quod aliquis conceptus est communis Deo et
omnibus aliis rebus.
63 Ad argumentum principale dico quod quamvis multa
sint primo diversa illo modo quo loquuntur auctores,
tamen de eis bene potest praedicari unus conceptus, et
66 univoce.

Notes

1. **praedicetur:** as a technical term of logic, 'predicated', from Boethius on, but it is a sense old enough
in Latin: cf. Plautus, *Am.* 1,1,249: *quod mihi prae-
dicabas vitium, id tibi est.*
univoce: *univocus,* 'having one meaning' is found
in Martianus Capella, as is *aequivocus,* 'having more

than one meaning', 'equivocal'. *Aequivocatio* (line 7) and the adverb must also go back to the same antique logical sources (Stoic?).

3. **primo:** presumably metaphysically rather than temporally: 'in principle'.

8. **teneo:** 'I maintain, defend'; cf. L.& S. s.v. I B 2 c.

9. **correspondet:** possibly a 13th-c. word for CL *respondere* (L.& S. s.v. II B), but it does look older.

12. **Sortes:** a sort of John Doe of medieval dialectic.

13. **tales vocales:** 'sounding thus'?.

17. **et aliquid:** i.e. not *nihil*.

18. **de veniente a remotis:** 'from an impression coming from far off'.

26. **simul et semel:** 'at one and the same time'.

30. **nec convertibile:** 'nor any less convertible with'.

33. **alius ab inferioribus:** *alius ab, absque* are found in the Old Latin and Vulgate Scriptures for 'different from'; *inferioribus* means lower in the logical 'tree', as *species* is lower than *genus*.
    communius: the text has here, without comment, *communis*.

39. **subicibilibus:** from *subicio* ; cited by Latham as 1270; another dialectician's coinage:'subordinate'.
    supponant: a term supposits (*supponit*) for that which it 'stands for', as distinguished from what it means (*significat*): the term 'man' signifies you and me and John Doe etc.; in the proposition 'man is a species' it has what Ockham calls 'simple supposition' (*suppositio simplex*), it clearly does not stand for you and me and etc., since neither you nor I nor John Doe is a species. The Nominalists said it did not signify anything except the mental term 'man', which is a specific term; the Realists maintained that it signified a <u>real</u> 'nature' man, human nature. A term has personal supposition (*supponit personaliter*) when it stands for what it signifies: in 'some man is white' it stands for this man or this one or..The third kind of supposition is material, as in 'man is a three-lettered word', or 'man is a common noun', where it stands for itself, the word spoken or written.

46. incomplexam: found in late Glossaries in the sense of 'incomprehensible', but in this literal sense it is possibly 13th-c.

50. intuitiva: 'by seeing', not 'intuitive'; literal, from *intueor*. A late 12th-c. word.

51. abstractiva: *abstractus* in the modern philosophical sense is used from 6th c. on, but this adjective seems to be 13th-c.

56. et habetur propositum: 'the proposition is established, proven'. For *habere* see L.&. S. s.v. II D 1.